The Hard Knock Life and The Real 'OG'

Build A Fortress Around Your Life

Pothen Manamel Cherian

INDIA • SINGAPORE • MALAYSIA

Copyright © Pothen Manamel Cherian 2024
All Rights Reserved.

ISBN 979-8-89133-807-4

This book has been published with all efforts taken to make the material error-free after the consent of the author. However, the author and the publisher do not assume and hereby disclaim any liability to any party for any loss, damage, or disruption caused by errors or omissions, whether such errors or omissions result from negligence, accident, or any other cause.

While every effort has been made to avoid any mistake or omission, this publication is being sold on the condition and understanding that neither the author nor the publishers or printers would be liable in any manner to any person by reason of any mistake or omission in this publication or for any action taken or omitted to be taken or advice rendered or accepted on the basis of this work. For any defect in printing or binding the publishers will be liable only to replace the defective copy by another copy of this work then available.

Table of Contents

Introduction

I still remember that pivotal moment in my life when everything changed. It was a gloomy day, rain pouring down as if the heavens themselves were weeping. I stood at the edge of the precipice, feeling the weight of the world on my shoulders, confused and lost but with a deep yearning for something more.

In that moment of despair, I found solace in an unexpected place. I turned to my faith, seeking answers from the Christian God. It was then that I discovered the concept of the "Real OG", the ultimate **Original Gangster** who had been there since the beginning, shaping destinies and guiding lives. This book is an exploration of the synergy between faith in the Christian God and empathy, and how our choices ultimately shape our destiny.

In a world driven by proof and empirical evidence, the concept of faith may seem outdated and illogical to some. Yet, within the Christian belief system, faith holds a central position. As Jesus himself said, "Blessed are those who have not seen and yet have believed." This notion of believing in something intangible, something that cannot be physically proven, holds immense power in shaping our lives.

Science, with its remarkable advancements and undeniable influence, has become the yardstick by which we measure our understanding of the world. However, when it comes to proving the existence of a spiritual being like God, science has its limitations. It is in this tension between faith and science that we find the true power of belief in the unseen. It is through faith that we open ourselves up to the possibility of a higher power, one that science alone cannot explain.

Our ability to feel and experience emotions is a testament to the complex nature of human existence. Science has yet to definitively explain the origin and purpose of emotions, yet we know that they play a significant role in our lives. This realization highlights the importance of trusting in our own experiences and intuition, even in the face of scientific uncertainty. We must navigate the contradictory nature of relying on science while valuing the profound impact of our relationships and connections with others.

The quest for truth and purpose is a universal pursuit that transcends religious boundaries. Even those who do not identify as believers still grapple with philosophical questions about existence. This search for truth and the discovery of one's purpose in life are noble endeavors that require hope and resilience. It is through this journey that we come to understand the importance of faith in guiding us toward a fulfilling life.

In our relentless pursuit of happiness, there is a temptation to remain willfully ignorant. We may choose to ignore the pursuit of knowledge and truth in favor of blissful ignorance. However, this path comes at a great cost to our personal growth and understanding. We must question the notion that seeking knowledge and truth should be sacrificed for the sake of momentary happiness. Intellectual curiosity and the pursuit of truth are essential for our spiritual and intellectual development.

One does not need to be a believer to contemplate one's conscience and the deeper questions of existence. The quest for truth and our personal beliefs, regardless of religious affiliation, allows us to deepen our understanding of ourselves and our place in the world.

For me, Christianity holds the answers I have been searching for. The concept of God's sacrifice through sending His only son exemplifies the true essence of love. It is through this act that Christianity becomes more than just a religion, but a faith that requires belief in God's sacrifice as an expression of love. This belief shapes our understanding of empathy and guides us toward a life of purpose and fulfillment.

I am born a human being and I choose to be a Christian. As a person who at birth is void of any labels philosophically speaking, we have chosen one specific task. This question, so to speak, rings clear like a death knell and we are confronted by it at many points down life's long road: What kind of person do I want to be?

In one of my classes at college, I was introduced to the concept of being a 'conscious being'. As human beings, we make choices that affect our lives either in a good way or a bad way. I am not saying that life is black and white, but I believe that if at the end of life when we are at death's door, a person who has run his race well would be content while a person with regrets will find it difficult to reach that same contentment. Stuck at home during the Covid quarantine I have had a lot of time to myself and since my past seemed to be drenched with failure and not living up to expectations, I told myself that in the pursuit of self-realization, perhaps writing would offer me some catharsis.

Belief in God is a very personal choice. Sometimes it may seem to us that we need no evidence but that we need to have hope. Hope that there is something beyond this life and that we are conditioning ourselves in preparation for something profound. Faith in Jesus Christ and his sacrifice for us is one of the cornerstones of Christianity. However, belief is personal and faith is about making a commitment to hold ourselves to higher standards to imbibe self-respect before expecting other people to treat us with respect, 'love your neighbor as yourself'. The mental image of turning the other cheek is similar to the theological image of Jesus asking God to forgive humanity for killing him and they speak to wisdom that should be nurtured in our values.

Embarking on my journey of self-exploration and spiritual growth, I realized that in order to become the person I aspire to be, I needed to attain a profound understanding of myself at a fundamental level. While I had an understanding of my preferences, social circles, and interests, there existed a deeper realm of self-awareness that remained uncharted.

Armed with curiosity, I took a step in faith and set off on my journey to fathom how my benevolent heavenly Father perceives me. I believe that comprehending the Father's perception of me will ultimately shape my own perception of who I am. I realized that I had subconsciously neglected introspection regarding my own sense of self and, in turn, failed to acknowledge my innate desire to evolve and surpass my current state.

In this book, I try to delve deeper into the exploration of faith and empathy, how our choices shape our destiny, and how for me, my faith can guide me toward living a fulfilling life. The concepts of belief in the unseen, the dilemma of science, the power of emotions and relationships, the search for truth and purpose, the risk of ignorance, conscience, and personal beliefs, the importance of kindness and love, and the glory of God's sacrifice will be explored and I invite you on this personal journey of self-discovery.

Chapter 1

Unveiling the Synergy Between Christian Beliefs and Who I Am

Discovering Hebron School

Hebron School holds a significant place in my life, a place where my curiosity about spirituality and the concept of God began. Nestled in the picturesque hills of Ooty, India, Hebron School stands as a beacon of education and enlightenment. With its sprawling campus and diverse student body, it provides a nurturing environment that encourages intellectual growth and spiritual exploration.

My first encounter with Hebron School was a moment of sheer fascination and wonder. As I stepped onto the campus for the first time, a rush of emotions swept over me. The air seemed charged with a sense of possibility and discovery. I couldn't help but be captivated by the aura of intellectual curiosity that permeated the place as if the very walls of the school whispered profound secrets of knowledge waiting to be unraveled.

As I immersed myself in the vibrant academic environment, I found myself questioning the nature of God and the intricacies of spiritual existence. The diversity of beliefs among my fellow students and the conversations we shared fostered a sense of intellectual inquiry that led me to explore the depths of my own spiritual beliefs.

My journey into spirituality took a deeper turn as I encountered various religious teachings within Hebron School. From the teachings of Christianity to the philosophies of Hinduism and Buddhism, I was exposed to a multitude of perspectives that challenged and expanded my understanding of the divine. The lessons learned within the classrooms and the conversations I had with teachers and classmates alike opened new pathways of thought and reflection.

As I delved deeper into spiritual ideas, doubts and questions began to emerge, and the more I explored, the more uncertainty I encountered. The complexities of the human experience and the existence of suffering seemed to clash with my initial understanding of a benevolent higher power. Wrestling with these uncertainties became a part of my daily existence, forcing me to confront the limits of my own understanding.

In my quest for answers, I embarked on a journey of self-discovery and exploration. I often attempted, to engage in meaningful conversations with individuals from various faith traditions, seeking wisdom and guidance.

The impact of Hebron School on my spiritual quest cannot be understated. It was at this school that I learned the value of questioning, of seeking truth even in the face of uncertainty. Through this journey, I have come to embrace the idea that curiosity is a catalyst for growth and intellectual evolution.

Engaging with different religious and philosophical ideas within Hebron School expanded my perspectives challenging my own biases and preconceptions. Encounters with other belief systems allowed me to embrace a more holistic understanding of spirituality and the concept of God, transcending the limitations of any single tradition.

My initial encounter with Hebron School and the curiosity it ignited continues to fuel my thirst for knowledge and understanding. Each new experience, each encounter with different perspectives, only serves to further stoke the flames of curiosity within me, propelling me forward on my journey of self-discovery.

The impact of Hebron School on my curiosity about spirituality has been profound. It has shaped not only my personal beliefs and intellectual development but also the way I engage with the world around me instilling a desire to approach life with an open mind and a willingness to embrace the unknown.

The Role of Worship

My early exposure to worship music was a profound and transformative experience. It began with attending church services as a child, where the melodies and lyrics washed over me like a gentle rain, soothing my soul and filling me with a sense of peace. The songs became a soundtrack to my spiritual journey, accompanying me through family gatherings, personal listening experiences, and moments of quiet reflection.

One particular song that left a lasting impression on me was 'Reckless Love' by Cory Asbury. Its powerful lyrics spoke of redemption and the unfathomable love of a higher power. As I listened to the Evocative melody, tears streamed down my face, and I felt an overwhelming sense of awe and gratitude. This was my first taste of the emotional impact that worship music could have on me.

Worship music has the unique ability to stir the deepest emotions within us, to transport us to a place beyond the physical realm, where our spirits are free to soar. For me personally, singing and engaging with worship music evoked a sense of joy that bubbled up from within. The lyrics and melodies resonated with my soul, touching something deep and intangible.

In those moments of listening to worship music, I felt a profound sense of peace. It was as if all my worries and anxieties were washed away and replaced by a calm assurance that everything would be okay. The music became a balm for my weary soul, a refuge in the chaos of life.

My exposure to worship music planted the seeds of a deeper connection with spirituality. As I listened to the songs, I began to sense a presence beyond myself, a higher power that reached out and embraced me. The music became a conduit for this connection, allowing me to explore my faith in ways I had never imagined.

I found myself craving more of these transcendent moments, longing to dive deeper into the mysteries of spirituality. The music became a gateway, leading me down a path of self-discovery and spiritual growth. I began to seek out other forms of worship music, exploring different genres and styles, each one offering a unique perspective on faith and spirituality.

One of the aspects of worship music that resonated deeply with me was its themes. Love, surrender, redemption, and hope were recurring motifs in the songs that spoke to me on a profound level. For example, the song "How Great Thou Art" captured the awe and wonder I felt when contemplating the majesty of a higher power. The lyrics transported me to a place of reverence and humility, reminding me of my place in the grand tapestry of life.

As I delved deeper into the themes of worship music, I began to see how they mirrored my own journey of personal growth and transformation. The music became a reflection of my own experiences, a source of inspiration and guidance as I navigated the challenges of life.

My connection with worship music led to personal growth and transformation. It influenced not only my thoughts and beliefs but also my actions in the world. The songs became a reminder of the values I held dear, urging me to live a life of love, compassion, and service to others.

Through worship music, I found solace in times of sorrow, strength in moments of weakness, and inspiration when I needed it most. It became a constant companion, accompanying me through the highs and lows of life. The transformative power of worship music shaped my understanding of surrender and deepened my relationship with God.

Despite the profound impact of worship music on my spiritual journey, I also faced challenges and doubts along the way. There were moments when I questioned my beliefs, wrestled with conflicting ideas, and struggled to find a sense of belonging within my faith community.

In those moments, the music became a lifeline, grounding me in the midst of uncertainty. It reminded me that it was okay to have doubts, to question, and to seek answers. Worship music became a space where I could grapple with the complexities of faith, finding comfort in the melodies and lyrics that had touched my soul.

The climax of my spiritual journey came during a worship service that left an indelible mark on my soul. It was a gathering of believers, all united by a common purpose—to connect with a higher power through music. As the worship band played, the room filled with electric energy, and I could feel the presence of something greater than myself.

At that moment, I was transported to a place of pure transcendence. The music swelled around me, wrapping me in its embrace, and I felt a deep sense of oneness with the universe. It was as if time stood still, and I was caught in the current of something divine.

Since that pivotal moment, worship music has continued to shape my life and spirituality. It remains an integral part of my spiritual practices, a wellspring of inspiration that stirs my soul and deepens my connection with a higher power. The songs continue to remind me of the power of love, the importance of surrender, and the hope that resides within each one of us.

Worship music has become a compass, guiding me through the twists and turns of life. It offers solace in times of uncertainty, inspiration in moments of doubt, and a reminder of the beauty that exists within and around us. It is a reminder that we are all connected, part of something greater than ourselves.

I am thankful for the artistes who pour their hearts and souls into creating worship music that touches lives and stirs hearts. Their dedication and talent have brought light into the darkest corners of my being, reminding me of the power of music to heal, uplift, and transform.

(As I reflect on my own journey with worship music, I invite you, dear reader, to explore the power of worship music in your own life. Worship music has a special place in my heart as I believe that it provides an avenue through which we can establish a more intimate connection with the Father.

Take a moment to reflect on the songs that have touched your soul, the melodies that have stirred your emotions, and the lyrics that have inspired you. Allow them to guide you on your own spiritual journey, to deepen your connection with a higher power, and to remind you of the beauty that resides within and around you. Let the melodies and lyrics be a source of comfort, inspiration, and solace as you navigate the complexities of life.

May the power of worship music continue to stir your soul and lead you to a deeper understanding of yourself and the world around you.)

Who Am I?

I have reiterated my background toward the making of this book and the beginnings of my transformative journey. However, I am going to back up for a second because I think it is important that you have a little bit of a back story. My friends and family call me Sameer but my official name is Pothen. Sameer is a bit of a nickname. In our family, the first-born son takes the name of his paternal grandfather. A bit arbitrary to an outsider, but for me I think of it as me having direct access to the stories of who he was as if I could go to sleep one night, and see what he was like in life. Furthermore, and possibly more importantly, it provides me with a direct connection to what my forefathers have worked so hard to build.

From a young age, I loved music. I mean I often used to imagine what it would be like if I were on a stage performing and if the song I was listening to on my iPod was a song I actually composed. I enjoyed a variety of music particularly influenced by the songs my dad played in the car. I slowly started to develop a fascination for country and rock & roll.

Later on, I was influenced by a close family friend who I have always considered as an older brother when he freestyled for me. I still remember that day; before then I hardly had an appreciation for rap and I knew that he used to engage in it, but at that moment, for the first time, I had a front-row seat to what I could only in my state of captivation describe as a 'wild performance'. He always used to tell me that rap was just expression and that you don't always need to think too much, but I knew very early on that it was important not to do it just to sound cool but that you need to strive to be an authentic musician who respects the art-form.

Why Faith Matters

Faith, the invisible force that shapes our lives, is a subject of great significance and relevance. It is the guiding light that illuminates our paths, providing us with hope, purpose, and a deeper understanding of the world around us. In this chapter, I aim to explore the multifaceted nature of faith, highlighting its role in shaping our perspectives and actions.

To truly understand the power of faith, we must first grasp its essence. Faith can be defined as a steadfast belief in something or someone, regardless of tangible evidence. When a person has faith in themselves, to me, it represents the idea that you believe that God can work through you to bring about good things. It is an unwavering trust that transcends the limitations of what can be seen or proven. Through faith, we tap into a realm beyond our senses, where hope and meaning intertwine.

In our darkest hours, faith acts as an anchor, providing strength and comfort when all else seems lost. It allows us to navigate through life's challenges with resilience and grace. The belief in a higher power or our unique purpose offers solace and the assurance that we are never truly alone in our struggles. Faith, in its essence, is a beacon of light that guides us through the storm.

However, it is not uncommon for skepticism to arise when discussing faith. Many argue that without physical proof, faith is merely a coping mechanism, an illusion we create to alleviate our fears and uncertainties. While acknowledging this skepticism, we must recognize the limitations of relying solely on physical proof. The realm of faith is not bound by scientific evidence; it is a realm of the heart and soul.

The blessings of faith extend far beyond the need for physical proof. Faith, in its purest form, opens doors to personal experiences and transformations that are often unattainable through mere logic and reasoning. It enables us to tap into our inner potential, to discover strengths we never knew we possessed. Faith brings about a sense of interconnectedness with the universe, leading to a deep sense of fulfillment and purpose.

In a world driven by materialism and skepticism, the importance of faith cannot be overstated. It is a force that shapes our perspectives and actions, giving us hope and meaning in the face of adversity. While skepticism may persist, the blessings of faith are undeniable. Through faith, we find strength, comfort, and personal growth.

It is in the embrace of faith that we uncover the true essence of our existence, the real "OG" within ourselves.

The Importance of Faith in Different Religions

Faith, the cornerstone of many religions worldwide, serves as a beacon of guidance, purpose, and solace for believers. In this chapter, we shall delve into the profound importance of faith across various religions, including Christianity, Islam, Hinduism, Buddhism, and Judaism.

5.1.1: Faith in Christianity

Christianity views faith as an indispensable element for salvation and establishing a personal connection with the divine. By placing their faith in Jesus Christ, Christians believe they can attain absolution of sins and everlasting life. Faith, in this context, acts as a transformative force, enabling adherents to align their lives with the teachings of Jesus and experience spiritual growth. The Bible, the holy scripture of Christianity, extensively underscores the weight of faith. For instance, Hebrews 11:1 resonates with the declaration that *"faith is the assurance of things hoped for, the conviction of things not seen."*

5.1.2: Faith in Islam

In Islam, faith takes on the name of "Iman" and represents one of the Five Pillars of the faith. Muslims embrace the belief in the unity of Allah (God) and the teachings of the Prophet Muhammad. Faith in Islam entails acknowledging Allah's existence, recognizing His attributes, and adhering to the guidance provided in the Quran. Through faith and submission to Allah's will, Muslims strive for spiritual purification and the attainment of Paradise.

5.1.3: Faith in Hinduism

Hinduism encompasses a vast tapestry of beliefs and practices, with faith acting as the vital thread that binds them together. Hindus place their faith in the existence of multiple deities, each embodying distinct aspects of the divine. Faith in Hinduism involves unwavering devotion to these deities, as well as belief in karma, the principle of cause and effect, and the cycle of reincarnation. Driven by their faith, Hindus embark on a quest for moksha, liberation from the perpetual cycle of birth and death.

5.1.4: Faith in Buddhism

Buddhism, often perceived as a philosophy rather than a religion, also accords significance to faith. Buddhists place their trust in the teachings of Gautama Buddha, who emphasized the Four Noble Truths and the Eightfold Path as the means to achieve enlightenment. Faith in Buddhism encompasses confidence in the Buddha's wisdom and guidance, as well as faith in one's own capacity to awaken to the truth and alleviate suffering.

5.1.5: Faith in Judaism

Within Judaism, faith is known as "Emunah" and serves as a cornerstone of the religion. Jews hold firm in their belief in one God and the divine covenant forged between God and the Jewish people. Faith in Judaism entails placing trust in God's promises and commandments, as well as faith in the arrival of the Messiah. Jewish faith finds expression through prayer, adherence to religious rituals, and unwavering commitment to ethical principles.

Ultimately, faith assumes immense significance across diverse religions, imparting believers with a profound sense of identity, purpose, and connection to the divine. It serves as a wellspring of strength and guidance, empowering individuals to navigate the tumultuous waters of life and find solace in their spiritual convictions. Whether through Christianity, Islam, Hinduism, Buddhism, Judaism, or any other religious tradition, faith remains an indispensable force, shaping the lives of adherents and fostering a profound comprehension of the divine.

The Power of Choice

I've always believed that our choices hold immense power. They have the ability to shape our character, determine our destiny, and ultimately define who we are. The decisions we make on a daily basis, no matter how small they may seem, have a direct impact on the path our lives take. It's through our choices that we have the power to create the life we truly desire.

Let's delve deeper into the influence of choices on our lives. Our decisions can lead us toward success or failure, happiness or misery. They are the building blocks that construct the foundation of our character and identity. Each choice we make reveals a glimpse of who we truly are. It is in these moments of decision-making that our true essence shines through.

In the midst of this discussion, I want to introduce the concept of following God's way as a guide for making choices. By aligning our choices with God's teachings and principles, we can experience a more fulfilling life. When we surrender our will to divine guidance, we tap into a higher power that guides us toward making choices that are in alignment with our highest good.

Yet, the journey of making choices is not always smooth sailing. We face numerous challenges and dilemmas along the way. Our desires often clash with God's will, and external influences can easily sway our decisions. It's in these moments that we truly test the strength of our character and our commitment to following God's way.

The consequences of our choices are significant. They have the power to shape not only our own lives but also those around us. Every choice we make sets off a chain reaction, leading us down a certain path. The immediate consequences may be evident, but it's the long-term impact that truly defines us. Our choices shape our character and destiny in ways we may not even realize.

Within the realm of choice, there are additional subtopics worth exploring. The concept of free will, for example, plays a crucial role in the power of choice. It is the freedom to make our own decisions that gives our choices their weight and meaning. Personal responsibility is another element to consider. We must take ownership of our choices and the consequences that arise from them. Lastly, the idea of divine intervention cannot be ignored. There are moments in our lives when we experience a higher power guiding our choices, offering us signs and synchronicities that lead us toward our true purpose.

At some point in our lives, we reach pivotal moments where our choices become critical. These moments test our commitment to following God's way. It's during these times that we must remember that the path of righteousness may not always be easy. It may require sacrifices and overcoming obstacles, but in the end, it leads to a greater sense of purpose and fulfillment.

It's important to acknowledge that we all make mistakes along the way. Our choices may lead us astray at times, but the key is to seek forgiveness and redemption. By acknowledging our mistakes and making amends, we can redirect our path toward a more fulfilling life. It's through the process of learning from our choices and growing from them that we find true resolution.

We have explored the significance of choices in defining our character and destiny. We've seen how our choices have the power to shape our lives, both in the immediate and long-term. By aligning our choices with God's teachings, we can experience a more meaningful and purposeful existence.

In conclusion, I want to reaffirm the notion that following God's way leads to a more fulfilling life. It is through the alignment of our choices with God's teachings that we tap into our highest potential. I encourage you, the reader, to reflect on your own choices and consider aligning them with God's teachings for a better future. The power of choice is in your hands, and by embracing it, you can create a life of purpose, joy, and fulfillment.

Questioning Faith

As I embarked on my journey of questioning faith, I quickly realized the immense significance it held for my personal growth and spiritual development. It was through this process that I began to truly understand myself and my beliefs on a deeper level.

Doubt, I discovered, played a crucial role in this process. It was through doubt that I was able to challenge my preconceived notions and beliefs and to truly examine the foundations of my faith. Rather than being a hindrance, doubt became a catalyst for a deeper understanding and a stronger relationship with God. It pushed me to seek answers, to question the status quo, and to ultimately arrive at a place of greater clarity and conviction.

Within religious communities, doubt often carries a negative connotation. It is seen as a sign of weakness or wavering faith. However, my exploration revealed a diverse range of perspectives on doubt. Some saw it as a sign of intellectual honesty and a necessary part of a robust faith. Others viewed it as a test of faith, a way to strengthen their relationship with God. These varying viewpoints enriched my understanding of doubt and challenged me to think beyond the confines of my own religious community.

As part of my journey, I also nurtured a curiosity pertaining to the stories of a few other religions and hence undertook an exploration of different religious traditions. I learned the importance of open-mindedness and empathy in understanding different faiths, and the role they play in fostering harmony and understanding among individuals of different religious backgrounds.

Of course, this journey was not without its challenges and obstacles. Questioning my faith often brought forth emotional and psychological turmoil. It forced me to confront deeply ingrained beliefs and to grapple with existential questions. Yet, it was through navigating these challenges that I grew stronger in my faith. I learned to lean on my support system, to seek guidance from mentors and trusted individuals who had walked a similar path. Their wisdom and encouragement provided me with the strength to overcome these hurdles and emerge with a renewed sense of purpose and conviction.

As I re-evaluated and re-discovered my personal beliefs, I found myself drawn to a new understanding of faith. It was a fluid and ever-evolving concept, influenced by a myriad of factors. The books I read, the conversations I had, and the experiences I underwent all played a role in shaping my new perspective. I came to realize the importance of individual interpretation, and the unique relationship each person has with God. No longer bound by rigid dogma, I found freedom in exploring and defining my own beliefs.

The role of the community in this journey cannot be understated. It can either be a source of support and understanding or a hindrance to individual faith exploration. The beliefs and norms of the community often shape our understanding of faith and can either encourage or discourage questioning. It was in finding a supportive and understanding community that I was able to thrive in my faith journey. Surrounding myself with like-minded individuals allowed me to freely explore my doubts and share in the joys and struggles of my spiritual growth.

The process of questioning faith also led me to re-evaluate theological concepts and doctrines. I critically examined these age-old beliefs, seeking a deeper understanding and clarity. Through this process, I gained theological insights that I had not previously considered. My perspective on God and the nature of divinity evolved, and I found myself embracing a more nuanced and inclusive theology.

Throughout this journey, I experienced profound spiritual transformations. My beliefs, practices, and understanding of God shifted in ways I had never anticipated. It was through this process of questioning that I was able to forge a more authentic and meaningful relationship with God. The depths of my faith were no longer defined by blind adherence but by a genuine and personal connection with the divine.

Embracing uncertainty and accepting the mysteries of faith became the cornerstone of my spiritual journey. I learned to acknowledge the limitations of human understanding and to find solace in the unknown. It was in embracing the uncertainties that I discovered the true essence of faith. It became a driving force in navigating the mysteries of God, a source of comfort in times of doubt and confusion.

Above all, this journey taught me the importance of cultivating a personal and unique relationship with God. I realized that God's presence and guidance in my life were not confined to religious institutions or dogmatic teachings. Rather, it was a deeply personal and individual experience. My faith journey continues to evolve, as I strive to deepen my understanding and connection with the divine. It is a journey that is ongoing, with each step revealing new insights and challenges to be overcome. Through it all, I am reminded of the profound significance of my personal relationship with God and the transformative power it holds.

Empathy as a Response to God

Empathy is a concept that holds immense significance in my belief system. It is not just an ordinary human emotion or a virtue; rather, it is a reflection of God's love. For me, empathy is a divine attribute that humans are capable of embodying. When we experience God's love, empathy becomes a natural response.

The broader theme that underlies the importance of empathy is treating others with kindness and equality. As humans, we have a responsibility to extend this love and kindness to our fellow beings. Empathy becomes the lens through which we see others as God sees them—with love and compassion.

Empathy, at its core, is the ability to understand and share the feelings of others. It goes beyond mere sympathy or pity; it is a deep and genuine connection to the emotions and experiences of another person. When we practice empathy, we are able to put ourselves in someone else's shoes, to see the world through their eyes.

But empathy is more than just a human characteristic; it is a divine quality that we can cultivate within ourselves. It is the bridge between human and divine love. When we empathize with others, we tap into a wellspring of compassion and understanding that mirrors God's love for us.

In my belief system, empathy is not just a passive emotion; it is an active response to experiencing God's love. When we feel the immense love and grace of God, it compels us to extend that love to others. Empathy allows us to see others as God sees them—as valuable, worthy beings deserving of love and compassion.

Empathy shapes my perspective on how I treat others with kindness and equality. It is a guiding principle that informs my interactions with those around me. By practicing empathy, I strive to embody God's love and extend it to every person I encounter.

God's love is a complex and profound concept, one that is difficult to fully comprehend. But empathy provides a glimpse into the nature of God's love. When we empathize with others, we tap into a small fraction of the vast love that God has for us. It is through empathy that we begin to grasp the depth and breadth of God's love.

In the teachings of the Bible, we find numerous examples that highlight the connection between empathy and God's love. Jesus, in his interactions with the marginalized and oppressed, demonstrated an unwavering empathy that was rooted in God's love. By examining these teachings, we can gain a deeper understanding of the role empathy plays in reflecting God's love.

Empathy plays a crucial role in enhancing relationships and fostering connections with others. When we empathize with someone, we are better able to understand their perspective and experiences. This understanding promotes forgiveness, reconciliation, and a deeper sense of connection.

By practicing empathy in our relationships, we break down barriers and promote unity. It allows us to bridge the gaps that exist between individuals and create a space where understanding and compassion can flourish. Empathy enables us to build strong and meaningful connections with others.

Empathy naturally leads to a perspective of treating others with equality. When we empathize with someone, we recognize and value their inherent worth and dignity. It becomes impossible to discriminate or marginalize when we truly understand and share in someone's experiences.

In a world that is often plagued by inequality and injustice, empathy has the power to bring about positive change. By cultivating empathy, we can contribute to creating a more just and inclusive society. It is through empathy that we can break down the walls that divide us and work toward a world where everyone is treated with fairness and respect.

Cultivating empathy requires intentional effort and self-reflection. It starts with self-awareness and active listening. We must be willing to step outside of ourselves and truly listen to the experiences and emotions of others. Perspective-taking is also essential in developing empathy. By trying to understand things from another person's point of view, we broaden our own understanding and capacity for empathy.

Practicing empathy goes beyond just understanding; it also involves taking action. Acts of kindness, service, and advocacy are tangible ways in which we can practice empathy. By extending ourselves to others and meeting their needs, we embody the love and compassion that empathy represents.

There are several barriers that can hinder our ability to empathize with others. Biases, prejudices, and self-centeredness can cloud our perspective and prevent us from truly connecting with others. Overcoming these barriers requires self-awareness and personal growth.

By cultivating self-awareness, we can identify our biases and prejudices and work toward overcoming them. It is through personal growth and a willingness to challenge our own beliefs that we can foster empathy toward others. By recognizing and actively working to overcome these barriers, we can create a space for empathy to thrive.

The transformative power of empathy is awe-inspiring. It has the ability to change not only individual lives but also entire communities. When we practice empathy, we open ourselves up to personal growth, healing, and the building of meaningful connections.

Empathy inspires us to look beyond ourselves and make a difference in the world. It has the potential to inspire positive social change and contribute to a more compassionate society. By cultivating empathy within ourselves and extending it to others, we can truly make a difference in the lives of those around us.

In conclusion, empathy is not just an emotion or a virtue; it is a reflection of God's love. It is a divine attribute that we, as humans, are capable of embodying. Empathy allows us to see others as God sees them, with love and compassion. It is through empathy that we can treat others with kindness and equality.

By understanding the concept of empathy, its connection to God's love, and its role in enhancing relationships, we can begin to cultivate empathy in our own lives. Through acts of kindness, self-reflection, and overcoming barriers, we can become more empathetic individuals. The transformative power of empathy has the potential to change lives and communities, and ultimately, create a more compassionate world.

Christianity as the Answer

For me, Christianity is not just a belief system; it is a deep conviction that I hold at the very core of my being. It is the answer to the questions that have plagued me for years and the foundation upon which I build my life. The significance of Christianity, particularly the sacrifice of God in Christ as an expression of love, has become clearer to me through a hypothetical scenario that I often reflect upon.

Imagine a world where love is scarce and genuine connections are rare. In this scenario, people are consumed by their desires and ambitions, often at the expense of others. The concept of sacrifice is foreign, and acts of selflessness are almost unheard of. It is a world where individuals are driven solely by their own self-interests, without any consideration for the greater good.

In this world, God decides to intervene and demonstrate the true meaning of love through sacrifice. He becomes human and experiences all the pain, suffering, and rejection that humanity has to offer. He willingly gives up his divine nature and takes on the frailty of a mortal life. This act of sacrifice is unprecedented and serves as a powerful symbol of love.

The scenario assumes that humanity, in its brokenness and selfishness, is unable to grasp the true meaning of love without a tangible example. God's sacrifice provides the ultimate example of selflessness, serving as a beacon of hope and redemption for those who choose to believe.

Choosing Christianity as the answer in this hypothetical scenario brings about a multitude of potential outcomes. It invites individuals to step out of their self-centered mindset and embrace a life of compassion, empathy, and sacrifice. By following the teachings of Christ, believers are encouraged to love one another as God has loved them.

God's sacrifice as an expression of love has profound implications in this scenario. It challenges the notion that love is only transactional and conditional, reminding individuals that it is a force that transcends personal gain. It serves as a reminder that love requires sacrifice, and in giving of oneself, true fulfillment and purpose are found.

Christianity provides guidance, purpose, and fulfillment in my own life. It offers a roadmap for navigating the complexities of existence and gives meaning to the mundane. Through my faith, I have discovered a sense of purpose that extends beyond my own desires and ambitions. It allows me to view my life as a vessel for God's love and to serve others in a way that brings true joy.

I believe in the transformative power of Christianity and its ability to bring hope and redemption to even the most broken individuals. It offers a path toward healing and restoration, enabling individuals to find forgiveness and a new beginning. This belief is not limited to a specific group or demographic but is a universal need for all humanity.

My personal experiences have only strengthened my conviction in Christianity as the answer. I have witnessed the transformational power of love in my own life and the lives of those around me. Through acts of selflessness and sacrifice, I have seen relationships mended, wounds healed, and lives transformed.

The significance of God's sacrifice as an expression of love has personally impacted me in profound ways. It has shown me that love requires action and that true love is not passive but actively seeks the well-being of others. It has taught me to value relationships over possessions and to find fulfillment in serving others.

In conclusion, Christianity is not just a belief system for me; it is a way of life. It offers a profound understanding of love, sacrifice, and purpose that has the power to transform lives. Through a hypothetical scenario and my own personal experiences, I have come to see the significance of God's sacrifice as the ultimate expression of love. It is through this sacrifice that hope and redemption are found, and a higher purpose in life is discovered.

The Tension Between Society and Faith

In today's fast-paced and ever-changing world, there exists a palpable tension between society and faith that deeply impacts individuals' lives. This tension arises from the conflicting messages society sends about success and opportunity, often leaving people torn between their religious beliefs and societal expectations. As someone who has experienced the trials and tribulations of navigating this tension first-hand, I understand the importance of staying true to one's faith in the face of societal pressures.

The societal definition of success frequently clashes with religious values, causing individuals to question their priorities and make difficult decisions. Society pressures us to conform to its norms, often leading us astray from our deeply held religious convictions. We find ourselves standing at the crossroads, torn between the pursuit of worldly success and remaining faithful to our beliefs. In these moments, it is crucial to reflect on the impact societal expectations have on shaping our opportunities and recognize the potential consequences of compromising our faith.

Family plays a significant role in our lives and can greatly influence our decision-making processes. However, conflicts can arise when family expectations clash with our religious beliefs. Navigating these challenges requires open communication and understanding within familial relationships. It is essential to foster an environment where differing viewpoints can be respectfully discussed, allowing for personal growth and the preservation of one's faith.

Friends also exert a powerful influence on our decision-making, often posing challenges to our religious convictions. Peer pressure can be overwhelming, tempting us to compromise our faith in order to fit in. Surrounding ourselves with supportive friends who respect and understand our religious beliefs is crucial. Such friendships provide a safe space to express our struggles and receive the encouragement needed to stay true to our faith, even in the face of adversity.

Staying true to one's faith is of paramount importance, regardless of the pressures exerted by society and peers. Faith serves as a guiding principle in decision-making, helping us navigate the complexities of life with clarity and purpose. Remaining steadfast in our beliefs may present challenges, but the potential rewards far outweigh the difficulties. By staying true to our faith, we develop a sense of inner strength, resilience, and peace that transcends the fleeting trends and expectations of society.

While society and faith often seem at odds, they can also intersect and influence each other in profound ways. Integrating religious values into society can lead to progress and positive change. By infusing our communities with compassion, empathy, and moral principles, we create a world that is more just and equitable. Striking a balance between societal expectations and religious convictions is crucial to effecting meaningful change while staying true to our faith.

Navigating the tension between society and faith can be a daunting task, but there are strategies to cope with the conflicting messages. Self-reflection and introspection play a vital role in navigating these tensions, allowing us to understand our values and priorities more deeply. Additionally, seeking support and guidance from our community helps us overcome challenges and provides a network of like-minded individuals who can offer advice and encouragement along the way.

The conflicting messages we encounter between society and faith can have a detrimental impact on our mental health. The constant pressure to conform and the internal struggle to reconcile our beliefs with societal expectations can lead to anxiety, stress, and even depression. Seeking professional help and support is crucial in such situations. Engaging in self-care practices and stress management techniques can also help maintain mental well-being and provide the necessary resilience to navigate these tensions.

Building a supportive network of individuals who share similar religious values is vital for maintaining faith in the face of societal pressures. Belonging to a religious community or support group provides a sense of belonging and understanding. These communities offer a space where we can share our struggles, find guidance, and receive the support necessary to navigate the tension between society and faith.

The long-term effects of navigating the tension between society and faith are profound. By staying true to our beliefs, we cultivate personal growth and resilience. We develop a deep sense of self-acceptance and find peace in the midst of conflicting messages. The journey of navigating this tension becomes a transformative process, allowing us to embrace our authentic selves and forge a path that aligns with our deepest convictions.

In conclusion, the tension between society and faith is a significant aspect of our lives that demands careful consideration. It requires us to navigate conflicting messages, make difficult decisions, and build a supportive network. By staying true to our faith, we not only preserve our own values but also contribute to societal progress and positive change.

The Concept of Love as the Ultimate Answer

Love, the ultimate answer, knows no bounds of religion and stands as a quintessential facet of human existence. In its purest form, love possesses an indomitable force that can metamorphose lives, mend wounds, and forge connections among people. It is a language universally understood, echoing the deepest yearnings of the human soul.

Christianity, at its core, places love as the bedrock of Jesus Christ's teachings. His followers were instructed to love unconditionally, to extend love to their neighbors as they would themselves, and astonishingly, even to their adversaries. The renowned verse from the Bible, 1 Corinthians 13:4-7, eloquently illustrates the attributes of love—patience, kindness, humility, selflessness, forgiveness, and endurance. I endeavor to embody these qualities, striving to love others as Christ loved them.

Islam similarly emphasizes the significance of love in the teachings of Prophet Muhammad. Muslims are encouraged to exhibit love and compassion toward their fellow human beings, to be magnanimous and benevolent, and to treat others with reverence and honor. The concept of brotherhood and sisterhood within Islam is founded upon the love and unity that believers ought to possess for one another.

Within Hinduism, love is perceived as an indispensable element of the path to spiritual enlightenment. Hindu scriptures, such as the Bhagavad Gita, delve into divine love and devotion. Bhakti, the path of love and devotion, stands as one of the primary routes toward achieving union with the divine. Through acts of love and devotion, I strive to establish this profound connection, basking in the bliss of divine love.

Buddhism accentuates the importance of cultivating love and compassion for all beings. The practice of loving-kindness, known as *metta*, constitutes a central tenet of Buddhist teachings. Buddhists are encouraged to nurture boundless love and compassion for all living creatures, transcending the barriers of self and others. By fostering love and compassion, I aspire to alleviate suffering and foster peace and harmony in the world.

In Judaism, love is intricately interwoven into the fabric of the faith. Jewish scriptures underscore the significance of loving God and loving one's neighbor. The commandment to love one's neighbor as oneself is deemed one of the greatest commandments in Judaism. Love is recognized as a potent force capable of metamorphosing lives and heralding redemption.

Beyond religious customs and traditions, love stands as a universal value that resonates with individuals from all walks of life. It possesses the power to bridge divides, heal wounds, and engender a more compassionate and harmonious world. Love transcends mere transient emotions, manifesting as a way of existence and interaction with others, rooted in kindness, empathy, and comprehension.

In a world often rife with division, animosity, and violence, the notion of love as the ultimate answer proffers hope and a vision for a brighter future. It implores individuals to surpass their differences and embrace love as a guiding principle in their lives. By cultivating love within our hearts and extending it to others, we can set forth a ripple effect capable of transforming not only our own lives but also the world that surrounds us.

In the forthcoming chapter, I will delve into the pragmatic ways through which love can be embodied in our daily lives and how it can generate positive change within ourselves and the world.

The Role of Prayer and Divine Intervention

In my quest for faith, I discovered the astonishing might of prayer and divine intervention in my ongoing skirmishes against the forces of darkness. Through fervent supplication, I discovered solace and guidance, forging an intimate connection with the Divine and encountering His presence in profound and extraordinary ways.

Prayer swiftly became my lifeline, a conduit to the divine that offered me strength beyond my own capacities. Amidst the depths of my struggles, I would pour out my heart to God in humble surrender. In my tears and petitions, I discovered solace, knowing that the Almighty was attentively listening, poised to bestow His love, support, and wisdom.

As I delved deeper into the practice of prayer, I realized that it was not a monologue, but an empowering exchange between myself and the divine. I learned to silence my thoughts and open my heart, allowing the comforting presence of God to flood me with peace, reassurance, and divine guidance.

Through prayer, I summoned the courage to confront the darkness lurking within me and overcome the sinister forces that attempted to hinder my journey. I bore witness to the transformative power of prayer, marveling at the miraculous intervention that catalyzed deliverance and healing.

Divine intervention played an indispensable role in my struggle against the forces of darkness. In moments of overwhelming turmoil, when seemingly insurmountable obstacles and impossible circumstances confronted me, I surrendered my fears and doubts to God, entrusting myself to the divine plan and providence.

Time and again, I marveled at the hand of God weaving through the tapestry of my existence. I experienced divine synchronicities, where fortuitous events converged harmoniously to orchestrate favorable outcomes. Supernatural protection enveloped me, shielding me from peril and danger through a force greater than my own being.

The divine intervention also materialized through divine appointments and encounters. At this precise juncture, individuals entered my life, imparting words of encouragement, support, and guidance. These encounters served as poignant reminders that I was not alone in my odyssey, that every detail was meticulously orchestrated by God to guide me toward triumph.

Through the transformative power of prayer and divine intervention, I discovered an unwavering resilience and tenacity. I learned to place my trust in the might of God, understanding that the Almighty fought alongside me in my battles against darkness. Prayer became my formidable weapon, and divine intervention my shield.

As I continue to pen the pages of my book, I remain resolute in my conviction that prayer and divine intervention are not abstract concepts, but living realities capable of transforming lives. I ardently hope that my words will inspire and empower others to embark on their own journey of faith, discovering the boundless power of prayer and the miraculous intervention of God in their own battles against darkness and malevolent forces.

And so, fueled by an intense desire to know God and a fervent desire to share the truth of my experiences,

I soldier on creating an intricate tapestry of hope, resilience, and ultimately victory.

Embracing the Call to Be a Prophet

At one point of significance in my journey, I had been struck by a divine revelation – God had called me to be a prophet. Initially, I had approached this calling with a mixture of uncertainty and caution, fully aware of the weightiness of such a unique role. As I engage with scriptures and earnestly seek divine guidance through prayer, the enormity of this task gradually becomes more manageable.

I set out on a challenging expedition to uncover the true essence of being a messenger. Contrary to common assumptions, it does not involve predicting the future or performing awe-inspiring feats. Rather, it entails acting as a conduit for conveying divine messages, embodying timeless truths in a world overshadowed by confusion and darkness.

Each passing day fueled within me a growing desire to share profound truths and love with those around me. I realized that this calling extends beyond mere message delivery; it requires living a life that mirrors the attributes of the divine, a source of hope in a fractured world.

However, my acceptance of this role does not come without trials and difficulties. Skeptics and doubters question the authenticity of my calling, attempting to undermine my unwavering faith. Yet, I stand firm, drawing strength from the unwavering dedication of those who have walked this path before me. Their words offer comfort and inspiration, reminding me that I'm not alone on this journey.

Throughout this expedition, I aspired to attempt to grasp the vital importance of discernment and humility. I have come to understand that being a messenger isn't about personal glory or gain. Instead, it's about surrendering to a higher will, faithfully delivering messages, no matter how challenging they may be.

As I persist in following this divine calling, I know I will witness the transformative power of these messages in the lives of those I encounter.

Within the pages of this unique book, I have candidly shared personal experiences, enlightening revelations, and invaluable lessons from my journey as a messenger.

Through each chapter, I have woven together captivating tales of divine moments, breathtaking revelations, and the lasting influence of these messages. With authenticity, I hope to inspire readers to boldly embrace their own paths, regardless of their nature, and to live out the profound truths and love that underlie existence.

As I continue to pour my energy into this book, my unyielding dedication to sharing experiences and insights becomes evident. I understand that the path of faith isn't always smooth, yet I firmly believe that with prayer, divine intervention, and a deeper connection with the divine, anyone can overcome challenges and uncover purpose in their lives.

"The Hard-Knock Life and The 'Real OG'" transcends being a mere faith-oriented book; it stands as a testament to the transformative power of divine love and human potential. It's a call to step beyond our comfort zones, embrace individual callings, and become messengers in our unique lives.

As I invest my heart and soul into these pages, I hope they serve as a guiding light for those seeking answers, meaning, and a positive impact. Through my words, I aim to empower readers to fearlessly embark on their own journeys of faith, embracing their roles with confidence and becoming the messengers they were meant to be.

Chapter 2

Shifting Priorities

Rekindling Passion

Growing up, I was always told to follow a certain path. Go to school, get good grades, find a stable job, and settle down. Society had its expectations, and I fell right into line. But as I got older, I couldn't shake the feeling that there was more to life than just going through the motions. I yearned to break free from these societal molds and rekindle the passions that had long been dormant within me.

For as long as I can remember, I've always had a deep love for music and writing. As a child, I would spend hours lost in my own little world, strumming away on a beat-up guitar or scribbling stories in tattered notebooks. But as I entered adulthood, these passions were stifled by the pressure to conform. Society told me that pursuing a creative path was unrealistic and risky.

So, like so many others, I buried my dreams and settled for a more conventional career.

But as the years went by, a sense of longing began to gnaw at me. I couldn't ignore the fact that I was living a life devoid of passion and purpose. And so, with a newfound determination, I embarked on a journey to rediscover these dormant passions and reclaim my true self.

Society has a way of placing us in boxes, dictating what we can and cannot do. It tells us that we must fit into predefined roles and adhere to certain expectations. These molds are suffocating, limiting our potential and stifling our individuality. They had kept me from pursuing my passions for far too long.

The impact of these molds on my sense of self and fulfillment was profound. I felt like a square peg trying to fit into a round hole, constantly at odds with who I truly was. I knew deep down that I had so much more to offer the world, but I was held back by the fear of stepping outside the boundaries that society had imposed upon me.

To truly understand the power of breaking free from societal molds, we must look to history for guidance. The Renaissance period serves as a remarkable parallel to my own journey of rediscovery. During this transformative era, individuals shattered the constraints of society and pursued their passions with unbridled enthusiasm.

Artists like Leonardo da Vinci and Michelangelo pushed the boundaries of creativity, defying societal norms and embracing their true artistic calling. Their boldness and refusal to conform paved the way for a new era of artistic expression, forever changing the course of history.

The Beat Generation, another historical parallel to my journey, emerged as a countercultural movement in the mid-20th century. Individuals like Jack Kerouac and Allen Ginsberg rebelled against the conformity of post-war America, seeking freedom and self-expression.

In their pursuit of personal truth, the Beat poets rejected societal norms and embarked on a journey of self-discovery. Through their poetry, literature, and jazz music, they found solace in the embrace of their passions. They dared to challenge the status quo and carved out their own paths, inspiring generations to come.

Reflecting on the experiences of the Renaissance period and the Beat Generation, I see patterns emerging. Both eras were marked by a rejection of societal expectations and a deep yearning for personal fulfillment. These individuals understood that true happiness could only be found by pursuing their passions wholeheartedly, regardless of societal judgment.

As I relate these historical parallels to my own journey, I am struck by the relevance and the lessons they hold. They serve as a reminder that breaking free from societal molds is not only possible but necessary for true fulfillment. They teach us that by embracing our passions, we can unleash our full potential and leave a lasting impact on the world.

Rekindling my dormant passions has been nothing short of transformative. It has breathed new life into my existence and reignited the fire within me. The impact on my sense of fulfillment and personal growth cannot be overstated. By breaking free from societal molds, I have been able to tap into a wellspring of creativity and authenticity.

No longer bound by the constraints of societal expectations, I have embraced my love for music and writing with unapologetic fervor. This newfound sense of purpose has given me a renewed zest for life and a deep sense of fulfillment that I had long been missing.

My journey of rekindling passion and breaking free from societal molds is far from over. It is a lifelong pursuit, an ongoing dance between self-discovery and personal growth. As I continue on this path, my future aspirations become clearer.

I envision a life where I can fully immerse myself in my passions, where my creativity knows no bounds. I dream of inspiring others to break free from societal constraints and embrace their true calling. Whether through my music, my writing, or simply leading by example, I aim to create a ripple effect of passion and authenticity in the world.

In conclusion, the historical parallels between the Renaissance period and the Beat Generation offer valuable insights into the power of rekindling passion and breaking free from societal molds. By sharing my own journey of rediscovery, I hope to inspire others to embrace their dormant passions and forge their own paths. In doing so, we can all experience a life that is truly fulfilling and authentic.

Conformity Vs. Authenticity

I've always been fascinated by the dichotomy between conformity and authenticity. It's a topic that hits close to home for me, as I've grappled with the internal conflicts that arise from this choice. Society places a great deal of importance on conforming to its expectations, but at what cost? Is it worth sacrificing our true selves to fit into a predetermined mold? These are the questions that have plagued me throughout my life.

Societal expectations can be suffocating. We're bombarded with messages about how we should look, act, and think. From a young age, we're taught to conform, to blend in with the crowd. But what happens when we're forced to suppress our authentic selves in order to fit in? I've witnessed first-hand the impact of societal norms on individuals. It's disheartening to see people lose their true identities in an attempt to meet the expectations of others.

Internally, I struggle with this battle between conformity and authenticity. There's a constant tug-of-war within me, as I navigate the conflicting emotions and thoughts that arise from this choice. On one hand, there's the desire to conform, to avoid standing out and risking judgment or rejection. On the other hand, there's a deep longing to embrace my authentic self, to live in alignment with my true values and beliefs. It's a constant struggle, but one that I believe is worth fighting.

Embracing authenticity is of utmost importance. When we live authentically, we experience a sense of self-confidence and fulfillment that can't be achieved through conformity. We attract genuine relationships, where others accept us for who we truly are. It's a liberating feeling to shed the mask of conformity and embrace our true selves.

However, the fear of judgment and rejection can be paralyzing. It's no easy feat to choose authenticity when the world tells us otherwise. I've personally experienced the fear and anxiety that comes with stepping outside societal norms. It takes courage to challenge the status quo, to go against the grain. But I've also witnessed the incredible impact of authenticity on those who have dared to be themselves. They inspire others, they break down barriers, and they create positive change in the world.

Choosing authenticity is a journey of self-discovery and self-acceptance. It requires introspection, reflection, and a willingness to confront our deepest fears and insecurities. Through this process, I've gained valuable insights about who I truly am and what I value most in life. It's a continual process of growth and learning, but one that is immensely rewarding.

Navigating relationships and social dynamics can be tricky when choosing authenticity. It requires open communication, setting boundaries, and finding a balance between staying true to oneself and respecting others. It's not always easy, but it's worth it to have relationships based on authenticity and mutual respect.

Finding support systems and resources is crucial on this journey. Surrounding ourselves with like-minded individuals, seeking out mentors, or even professional help can provide the guidance and encouragement needed to stay true to ourselves. It's important to know that we're not alone in this pursuit of authenticity.

Ultimately, embracing authenticity has the power to inspire and empower others. By sharing our own experiences and strategies for choosing authenticity, we can help others on their own journeys of self-discovery and self-acceptance. Positive and authentic change generates a healing ripple effect.

In conclusion, the choice between conformity and authenticity is a deeply personal one. It's a choice that requires courage, self-reflection, and a willingness to face our fears. But by embracing our authentic selves, we can experience a sense of freedom, fulfillment, and genuine connection that is worth fighting for.

The Courage to Be

In this subchapter, I want to share my journey toward embracing courageous authenticity. It has been a profound and transformative experience, and I believe it is essential for anyone seeking true fulfillment and happiness. Throughout my reflections, I have come to understand the challenges I faced and the importance of self-acceptance in this process.

As I embarked on this journey, I encountered numerous obstacles that tested my resilience. Society constantly bombards us with expectations and pressures to conform, and it takes immense courage to resist these external forces and embrace our true selves. Self-acceptance became a vital pillar in my pursuit of courageous authenticity, as I learned to embrace my flaws and imperfections rather than hide them away.

To illustrate the concept of embracing one's true identity, let me introduce you to a fictional character named Alex.

In the heart of a bustling city, amidst the cacophony of hurried footsteps and honking cars, there lived a young woman named Alex. She was, by all outward appearances, a reflection of the societal norms that enveloped her world. Her attire was meticulously chosen to match the latest fashion trends, her speech tailored to blend seamlessly with the conversations around her, and her aspirations aligned with the expectations of her family and peers.

Yet, beneath the facade of conformity, there existed a profound disquiet within her: a dissonance that tugged at her soul and whispered a truth she had long been suppressing. Alex had, over the years, hidden her true self, stifling the passions and quirks that defined her uniqueness. She lived her life through the lens of societal expectations, choosing conformity over authenticity.

The world saw a polished, composed woman, but deep within, Alex felt like a fractured mirror, reflecting a distorted image of her true identity. The fear of judgment, rejection, and societal scrutiny had driven her to suppress the very essence of who she was. The consequences of this self-denial were severe, for she had become a mere echo of her own potential.

Each day, as she navigated the maze of her existence, Alex felt a growing sense of emptiness. Her emotional well-being suffered, as her heart yearned to break free from the chains of conformity and dance to the rhythm of her own desires. She was disconnected from her own spirit, lost in a sea of expectations that drowned her individuality.

It was on one fateful day, as she stood by the window of her sterile apartment, gazing at the cityscape below, that a revelation struck her like a bolt of lightning. The facade she had built over the years was suffocating her, and she could no longer deny the yearning within her to embrace her true self.

Alex embarked on a journey of self-discovery, guided by the beacon of her authentic desires. She delved into her long-neglected passions, uncovering talents she had never dared to nurture. She rekindled the creative fire that had smoldered within her, creating art that was a testament to her unique vision.

As she began to express her true self, the world around her reacted in ways she had feared, with raised eyebrows and questioning glances. But Alex had found a wellspring of courage deep within her, and she refused to bow to the judgments of others. She knew that her authenticity was worth the price of societal discomfort.

With each step toward embracing her true identity, Alex felt a profound sense of liberation. She reconnected with her own spirit, finding a profound sense of fulfillment and inner peace. The dissonance that had once plagued her was replaced by a harmonious symphony of self-acceptance and genuine happiness.

In time, those who had once questioned her choices began to see the radiant authenticity that now defined Alex. Her courage inspired others to confront their own fears and embrace their true selves. The city that had once seemed cold and unforgiving began to warm to the beauty of individuality, one person at a time.

In the story of Alex, we find a profound lesson on the transformative power of embracing one's true identity. It is a reminder that the path to self-discovery may be daunting, but the rewards are immeasurable. For when we have the courage to be authentically ourselves, we not only find inner peace but also inspire those around us to do the same, creating a world that celebrates the rich tapestry of human diversity.

Alex's struggles in conforming to societal expectations are all too relatable. She constantly battles with the fear of not being accepted for who she truly is. Her journey is plagued with self-doubt, anxiety, and a constant sense of dissatisfaction. The weight of living a lie becomes unbearable, and she longs for a way out.

However, there comes a turning point in Alex's life, a moment of realization that propels her toward embracing her true identity. This catalyst could be a supportive friend who sees beyond her facade or a life-changing event that forces her to reassess her priorities. Whatever the catalyst may be, it sparks a fire within her, igniting a desire for change.

Embracing authenticity is not an easy path. It requires immense courage to let go of societal expectations and fully embrace one's true identity. Alex slowly begins to shed the layers of pretense, allowing her authentic self to shine through. With each step she takes toward self-acceptance, she experiences a profound shift in her sense of self-worth and overall happiness.

Of course, living authentically comes with its fair share of obstacles. Alex faces societal pressures and judgment from those who are uncomfortable with her newfound authenticity. However, she learns to navigate through these challenges with grace and resilience. She finds solace in the realization that her worth is not defined by others' opinions but by her own self-perception.

Through Alex's journey, I have learned valuable lessons about embracing courageous authenticity. It is a lifelong process that requires constant self-reflection and a commitment to growth. Self-acceptance is the key that unlocks the door to liberation and true fulfillment. It is only when we embrace our true identity that we can live a life aligned with our values and purpose.

The implications of Alex's journey extend far beyond her fictional world. It serves as an inspiration and encouragement for readers to embark on their own journey toward embracing their true identity. Each of us has a unique story to tell, and it is by embracing our authentic selves that we can create a life of meaning and impact.

In conclusion, I invite you to reflect on your own journey toward embracing courageous authenticity. What societal expectations have held you back? How can you cultivate self-acceptance and let your true self shine through? This subchapter is just the beginning of your exploration, and I encourage you to seek further resources and guidance on this transformative path. Embrace the courage to be, and watch as your life transforms in unimaginable ways.

From Limitations to Empowerment

I never thought I would be writing a book about my life, let alone one about philosophy. But here I am, ready to share my journey from self-imposed limitations to boundless empowerment. This subchapter is dedicated to exploring that transition and its significance in showcasing the strength and resilience that can be gained through conquering challenges.

For the longest time, I was held back by my own limitations. Fear, self-doubt, and negative self-talk were my constant companions. These self-imposed limitations prevented me from reaching my full potential. They were the chains that kept me confined, unable to explore the vast possibilities that lay beyond.

It wasn't until I faced a series of challenges that I was forced to re-evaluate these limitations. Life had a way of presenting me with situations and experiences that demanded I confront my fears head-on. It was sink or swim, and I chose to swim. These challenges became the catalyst for my transformation.

With each challenge, I discovered a reservoir of resilience and determination within myself. I broke free from the shackles of self-doubt and pushed through the barriers that held me back. Through these experiences, I grew as an individual, both personally and professionally. I learned to embrace the unknown and face adversity with unwavering strength.

Seeking empowerment became my primary goal. I sought therapy to unravel the layers of self-doubt that had built up over the years. Self-reflection became a daily practice, allowing me to uncover the root causes of my limitations. I also reached out to others for support, surrounding myself with individuals who believed in my potential.

As I embarked on this journey, I discovered hidden strengths and talents that had long been dormant. It was like uncovering buried treasure, and each new discovery fueled my sense of empowerment. I began to believe in my abilities and in the endless possibilities that awaited me.

Cultivating a positive mindset was key to my transformation. I had to reframe my thoughts and beliefs, replacing negative self-talk with words of encouragement and self-belief. I immersed myself in strategies and techniques that helped me shift my perspective and see the world through a more optimistic lens.

This transformative process was not easy. It required time, patience, and a commitment to personal growth. But through the challenges and the journey, I emerged stronger and more empowered than ever before. I realized that limitations were simply illusions, and that true growth could only be achieved by breaking free from them.

So why am I sharing this journey with others? Because I believe that my story has the power to inspire and impact those facing similar challenges. I want others to know that they too can break free from self-imposed limitations and find their own empowerment. By sharing my experiences, I hope to ignite a spark within others, motivating them to embark on their own transformative journeys.

Inspiring others is a responsibility I do not take lightly. I understand the importance of being a role model and showing others what is possible. My story serves as a powerful example, a testament to the strength of the human spirit and the capacity for growth and transformation.

In the end, it is my hope that this subchapter will not only provide insight into my own journey but also encourage readers to embrace their own potential. We all have the power to break free from self-imposed limitations and live a life of boundless empowerment. It is within each of us to redefine what is possible and rewrite our own narratives. The hard-knock life can be the catalyst for our transformation into a beautiful and authentic individual.

Chapter 3

Cultivating Benevolence

Nurturing Patience

Patience is a virtue that is often undervalued in our fast-paced and instant gratification-oriented society. In the context of personal growth and navigating challenges, patience plays a crucial role. It is the ability to endure and persevere in the face of adversity, without becoming overwhelmed or giving in to frustration. Patience allows us to cultivate resilience, learn from setbacks, and ultimately grow into better versions of ourselves.

When exploring the concept of patience, it is enlightening to turn to Eastern cultural perspectives, particularly those found in Buddhism and Taoism. These ancient traditions emphasize the importance of patience as a pathway to inner peace. Practices such as meditation and mindfulness are often used to cultivate patience and develop a calm and focused mind. In these philosophies, patience is seen as a virtue that enables individuals to accept the present moment without resistance, leading to a greater sense of harmony and tranquility.

In contrast, Western cultural perspectives on patience draw from examples in Christianity and Stoicism. Patience is often viewed as a virtue in Western societies, associated with virtues such as forbearance and self-control. It is through patience that individuals are encouraged to face adversity with resilience and maintain emotional well-being. Whether it is waiting for a job opportunity, dealing with a difficult person, or overcoming a personal setback, patience is seen as a tool for personal growth and character development.

A cross-cultural comparison of patience reveals both similarities and differences between Eastern and Western perspectives. Both cultures recognize the value of patience in navigating life's challenges, but they employ different approaches and practices to cultivate this virtue. Eastern cultures emphasize practices such as meditation and mindfulness, while Western cultures focus on self-control and perseverance. Cultural factors play a significant role in shaping the understanding and practice of patience, highlighting the diverse ways in which this virtue is valued and nurtured.

Real-life case studies provide compelling evidence of the transformative power of patience. Individuals from different cultural backgrounds have used patience to overcome challenges and achieve personal growth. Whether it is a Buddhist monk who spent years in meditation to cultivate patience or a stoic philosopher who faced adversity with unwavering resolve, these examples demonstrate the profound impact of patience on one's journey toward self-realization. These case studies serve as valuable lessons that can be applied to our own lives, inspiring us to embrace patience as a means to overcome obstacles and reach our full potential.

In our daily lives, we can apply patience in various situations to enhance our overall well-being. Practicing patience allows us to navigate conflicts with grace, build stronger relationships, and reduce stress. By embracing patience as a lifelong practice, we can experience personal and spiritual growth. In the midst of life's challenges and uncertainties, patience becomes a guiding principle that helps us maintain composure and find inner peace.

In conclusion, patience is a concept that holds great significance in personal growth and navigating challenges. Eastern and Western perspectives shed light on different approaches to cultivating this virtue, with both cultures recognizing its importance in achieving inner peace and resilience. Real-life case studies further highlight the transformative power of patience, inspiring us to embrace it in our own lives. By applying patience in everyday situations, we can enhance our relationships, reduce stress, and experience overall well-being. Patience is not just a fleeting virtue but a lifelong practice that can lead to profound personal and spiritual growth.

Divine Affection in Adversity

In the face of adversity, it is often our faith and belief in a higher power that provides solace and guidance. In this chapter, I want to explore the concept of 'Divine Affection' and its pivotal role in navigating life's hard knocks. For me, divine affection is not just a mere belief, but a profound understanding of the power of faith in dispelling fear and fostering personal growth. It is through this lens that I have come to view life's challenges as opportunities for growth and transformation.

Divine affection, in its essence, is the unconditional love and support we receive from a higher power. It is the belief that there is a divine force watching over us, guiding us through the toughest of times. This belief is not limited to any particular religion or spiritual tradition but is a universal concept that transcends boundaries. It is the understanding that we are never alone in our struggles and that there is always a higher purpose at play.

When we embrace divine affection, we open ourselves up to a new perspective on adversity. Instead of seeing challenges as insurmountable obstacles, we begin to view them as opportunities for growth and self-discovery. With faith as our guiding compass, we can navigate the stormy seas of life with resilience and inner strength.

To truly grasp the significance of divine affection in navigating adversity, let us consider some real-life examples and anecdotes. Take the story of Sarah, a single mother struggling to make ends meet. Despite facing financial hardships and constant uncertainty, Sarah found solace in her faith. Through prayer and unwavering belief in divine affection, she was able to find the strength to persevere. Her faith provided her with the guidance and comfort she needed to overcome each hurdle that came her way.

Another example is that of John, a cancer survivor. During his grueling battle with the disease, John turned to his faith for support. Through the power of divine affection, he found the strength to face his treatments with courage and determination. His faith not only gave him hope but also provided him with a sense of purpose in his journey toward healing.

It is through these stories and countless others that we can see the transformative power of divine affection. When we choose a life guided by faith, we are not only able to weather the storms of adversity but also emerge stronger and more resilient.

Some may argue that relying on divine affection in the face of adversity is unnecessary or ineffective.

They may question the role of faith in overcoming challenges and offer alternative approaches to navigating life's hard knocks. However, I believe that these alternative approaches often fall short of providing the same level of comfort, guidance, and growth that divine affection offers.

For instance, one alternative approach may be to rely solely on self-reliance and personal strength. While these qualities are undoubtedly important, they can only take us so far. In times of extreme hardship, it is often our faith that sustains us and provides us with the courage to keep going. Divine affection offers a sense of purpose and connection to something greater than ourselves, which can be a source of immense comfort and strength.

Furthermore, scientific studies have shown the positive effects of faith and spirituality on mental health and overall well-being. Research has indicated that individuals who have a strong sense of spirituality tend to experience lower levels of stress, depression, and anxiety. This suggests that choosing a life guided by faith and divine affection can have profound effects on our mental and emotional resilience.

Addressing potential criticisms or skepticism toward the concept of divine affection, it is important to acknowledge that faith is a deeply personal and subjective experience. What may resonate with one person may not resonate with another. However, it is through exploring our own beliefs and seeking a connection with a higher power that we can find meaning and purpose in the face of adversity.

In conclusion, divine affection plays a pivotal role in navigating life's hard knocks. By embracing faith and belief in a higher power, we open ourselves up to a new perspective on adversity. We no longer see challenges as roadblocks but as opportunities for growth and transformation. Through divine affection, we find comfort, guidance, and the strength to overcome even the most daunting of obstacles. It is through this lens that we can truly embrace the hard-knock life and become the real "OGs" of our own journeys.

Empathy as a Connection

Empathy is a powerful force that can bridge gaps between different human experiences and foster deep connections. It is the ability to understand and share the feelings of another person, allowing us to see the world from their perspective. In my book, "The Hard Knock Life And The 'Real OG'," I delve into the importance of empathy and how it can have a transformative impact on our lives and the world around us.

Empathy has the power to facilitate understanding between individuals. When we can empathize with someone, we can put ourselves in their shoes and truly comprehend their emotions and experiences. This understanding helps break down barriers and allows for more meaningful and compassionate interactions.

For example, imagine you're having a disagreement with a friend or family member. Instead of simply trying to prove your point or win the argument, empathy allows you to step back and truly understand their perspective. It opens the door to genuine dialog and helps create a space for resolution and compromise. By putting ourselves in their shoes, we can foster greater compassion and acceptance, leading to stronger relationships.

But empathy doesn't just stop at personal connections; it also plays a crucial role in healing on both individual and collective levels. When we feel understood and supported, it creates a sense of safety and allows for the healing process to take place. This can be particularly powerful in communities recovering from trauma or difficult experiences. Empathy can help individuals and communities come together, share their pain, and support one another in the journey toward healing and recovery.

In relationships, empathy strengthens bonds and connections. It allows us to truly listen and understand the needs and desires of our loved ones. By empathizing with their experiences, we can create a deeper and more meaningful connection. Empathy also helps resolve conflicts by allowing us to see the situation from the other person's perspective. This understanding promotes harmony and fosters an environment of trust and respect.

Empathy can also drive positive change in society. By embracing empathy, we can begin to truly understand and accept diverse perspectives. It breaks down the barriers that divide us and allows for greater collaboration and progress. Throughout history, empathy has been used to promote equality and justice, as individuals and communities have come together to fight for the rights of others. It is a powerful tool that can inspire collective action and create a better world.

Cultivating empathy is essential, and it can be developed and practiced in various contexts. Active listening is a key component of empathy, as it allows us to fully engage with and understand others. Engaging in empathy-building exercises can also help strengthen our empathetic muscles. Whether it's through role-playing or storytelling, these exercises allow us to step into someone else's shoes and expand our understanding of the world.

However, practicing empathy does come with its challenges. Empathy fatigue and burnout can occur when we constantly bear the emotional burden of others. It is important to establish boundaries and practice self-care to prevent these challenges from overwhelming us. Biases and preconceived notions can also hinder our ability to empathize. It is crucial to be aware of our own biases and actively work toward overcoming them in order to fully engage with others in an empathetic manner.

Empathy also plays a vital role in effective leadership. Empathetic leaders inspire trust and create positive work environments. By understanding the needs and motivations of their team members, empathetic leaders can guide and support them in reaching their full potential. There are numerous examples of empathetic leaders who have made a significant impact, from Mahatma Gandhi to Nelson Mandela. Their ability to empathize with the struggles of others allowed them to lead with compassion and create lasting change.

In a digital age where online communication is prevalent, fostering empathy can be a challenge. However, it is not impossible. By being mindful of our online interactions and actively promoting empathy in digital spaces, we can create a more compassionate and understanding online community. This may involve actively listening to others' perspectives, engaging in respectful dialog, and challenging our own biases and assumptions.

Looking toward the future, empathy will continue to play a crucial role in an increasingly interconnected world. As our world becomes more diverse and complex, empathy will be essential in fostering understanding and promoting positive change. Innovative approaches to empathy are already being utilized in various fields, such as healthcare and technology. These approaches help bridge gaps and create more inclusive and empathetic environments.

In conclusion, empathy is a potent force that can bridge human experiences, foster understanding, and facilitate collective healing. It is a call to action for all of us to actively embrace empathy in our lives. By doing so, we can create a more compassionate and connected world where everyone feels understood and supported. Let us all take up this call to action and practice empathy in every aspect of our lives.

Lessons for Life's Trials

Life is a journey filled with trials and tribulations that test our strength and resilience. It is during these difficult times that we truly discover who we are and what we are capable of. In this subchapter, I aim to provide you, the reader, with the tools and insights needed to navigate life's trials with grace and fortitude. It is my belief that by internalizing the lessons learned from our journey, we can not only survive but thrive in the face of adversity.

One of the key aspects of navigating life's trials is maintaining hope. It is easy to succumb to negativity and despair when faced with challenges, but by cultivating a positive mindset through prayer, we can approach these obstacles with a renewed sense of hope and optimism. Practicing gratitude is one powerful tool to help maintain a positive mindset: by acknowledging the things we are grateful for, and giving thanks to God, even when it seems like it may seem insignificant to God.

The truth is that no matter how small, showing gratitude by appreciating what we have rather than focusing on what we stand to gain is a way of opening our hearts to let God enter and empower our lives. Additionally, reframing negative thoughts can help us see challenges as opportunities for growth and learning. By changing our perspective, we can find silver linings even in the darkest of times. Real-life examples of individuals who have maintained a positive mindset in the face of adversity can inspire and motivate us to do the same.

Resilience is another crucial trait to develop when navigating life's trials. It is the ability to bounce back from setbacks and continue moving forward. Cultivating a support system is one effective strategy for building resilience. Surrounding ourselves with individuals who uplift and encourage us can provide the strength and motivation we need to persevere. Practicing self-care is equally important. Taking care of our physical and emotional well-being allows us to replenish our energy and face challenges with renewed vigor. Personal anecdotes and examples of individuals who have demonstrated resilience can serve as sources of inspiration and motivation.

Compassion, both toward us and others, is essential when navigating life's trials. By cultivating self-compassion, we can learn to accept ourselves as imperfect beings and forgive ourselves for our mistakes. This self-acceptance allows us to approach challenges with self-assurance and confidence. Showing compassion toward others is equally important. By actively listening to others and performing acts of kindness, we not only build strong relationships but also create a sense of interconnectedness that can provide comfort and support during difficult times.

Finding meaning and purpose amidst adversity can be a guiding light that helps us navigate life's trials. Setting goals and finding opportunities for personal growth can provide us with a sense of direction and motivation. Real-life stories of individuals who have discovered their purpose through challenging experiences can inspire us to seek our own purpose and meaning.

Managing stress is crucial when facing life's trials. Stress can negatively impact our physical and mental well-being, making it even more difficult to navigate challenges. Implementing practical stress management techniques, such as deep breathing exercises and effective time management strategies, can help us regain control and approach challenges with a clear and focused mind. Scientific studies and expert opinions can provide evidence of the effectiveness of these techniques, further emphasizing their importance.

Maintaining healthy relationships during challenging times is essential for support and guidance. Effective communication and conflict resolution skills are crucial for fostering healthy relationships.

By expressing our needs and emotions effectively, we can navigate challenges together and provide mutual support. Real-life examples and anecdotes can showcase the benefits of healthy relationships during difficult times, highlighting the importance of nurturing these connections.

Self-care is often overlooked in times of adversity, yet it is vital for our overall well-being. Prioritizing self-care and incorporating practices such as exercise and mindfulness into our daily routines can replenish our energy and provide us with the resilience needed to face challenges head-on. Real-life examples of individuals who have prioritized self-care and experienced positive outcomes can serve as inspiration for us to do the same.

Problem-solving and decision-making skills are invaluable when navigating life's trials. Breaking down complex problems into smaller, manageable steps can make daunting challenges more approachable. Seeking support and advice from others can provide fresh perspectives and insights that help us make informed decisions. Real-life examples and case studies can illustrate successful problem-solving and decision-making in difficult situations, inspiring us to develop and hone these skills.

Failure and setbacks are inevitable in life's trials, but it is how we bounce back from them that defines us. Reframing failures as learning experiences and maintaining a growth mindset can help us turn setbacks into opportunities for growth and improvement. Personal stories and examples of individuals who have overcome failure and achieved success can provide us with the motivation and inspiration to persevere.

In conclusion, navigating life's trials requires a combination of mindset, resilience, compassion, purpose, stress management, healthy relationships, self-care, problem-solving, and bouncing back from failure. By internalizing these lessons, we can not only survive but thrive in the face of adversity. I invite you to join me on this journey of self-discovery and growth as we learn to navigate life's trials with strength, grace, and resilience.

Chapter 4

The God Question

Belief in the Unseen

Belief in the unseen is a concept that holds profound significance across various religions and spiritual traditions. It is a belief that requires trust in something that cannot be empirically proven or observed. In a world that often values physical evidence and tangible proof, faith in the unseen offers a unique perspective and opens the door to a realm beyond our immediate senses.

Jesus, a central figure in Christianity, spoke about the blessedness of believing without physical evidence. These words hold particular weight in the story of Thomas, a disciple who doubted Jesus' resurrection until he could physically see and touch the wounds on Jesus' body. Jesus, however, responded by saying, "Blessed are those who have not seen and yet have believed."

This highlights the importance of faith, even in the absence of tangible evidence.

Belief in the unseen presents an ethical dilemma, as it requires navigating the tension between relying on physical evidence and having faith in what cannot be directly observed. In our modern society, where empirical evidence is often seen as the gold standard, making decisions or judgments based on what cannot be proven poses challenges. It raises questions about the legitimacy of relying on something intangible in a world that values concrete evidence.

From a rational perspective, belief in the unseen is often regarded as irrational and lacking a logical foundation. Those who hold this view argue that faith without empirical evidence is merely wishful thinking or blind acceptance. They emphasize the need for tangible proof and empirical evidence to support beliefs, dismissing the significance of faith as a subjective and unreliable basis for truth.

Contrary to the rational perspective, the spiritual approach views faith in the unseen as a deeply personal and transformative experience. It is seen as a means of connecting with a higher power and finding profound meaning in life. Faith becomes a journey of personal exploration and discovery, allowing individuals to transcend the limitations of the physical world and experience a deeper sense of purpose and fulfillment.

The consequences and impact of faith in the unseen extend beyond individual belief systems. It has the power to shape communities, fostering a sense of unity and shared values. However, relying on faith instead of physical evidence can also lead to blind obedience, potential manipulation, and the dismissal of critical thinking. Balancing the benefits and drawbacks of faith in a world that demands tangible proof is a constant challenge.

Believing in what is not physically seen can be met with numerous challenges and doubts. Internally, individuals may grapple with questions of credibility, authenticity, and the reliability of their own beliefs. Externally, societal pressures and skepticism can question and undermine one's faith. These challenges can fuel a constant battle within oneself and with the world, requiring resilience and introspection.

Despite the challenges, faith in the unseen can contribute to personal growth, resilience, and character development. It encourages individuals to confront doubts, fears, and uncertainties, fostering a sense of inner strength and resilience. Faith provides a source of hope, enabling individuals to navigate challenging times and find meaning amidst adversity.

Belief in the unseen is not exclusive to any particular religion or spiritual tradition. Examples abound across different cultures and contexts. From the belief in divine providence in Christianity to the concept of karma in Hinduism, faith takes various forms and expressions. Each tradition offers unique insights into the human experience, demonstrating how faith manifests differently across different cultural and religious practices.

Faith in the unseen remains a timeless and relevant topic in a world that often prioritizes physical evidence and empirical proof. It challenges us to embrace the unknown, navigate ethical dilemmas, and confront our doubts. Whether viewed through a rational lens or a spiritual perspective, faith offers a profound opportunity for personal growth, resilience, and connection with something beyond the physical realm. Its ongoing significance in our lives cannot be underestimated, as it continues to shape our individual beliefs and collective understanding of the world.

The Beauty and Mystery of Life

Life, oh life. It is a wondrous, transient thing. Its fleeting nature, like the delicate petals of a flower that bloom only to wither away, is what makes it so captivating. Science, with all its advancements and discoveries, has yet to disprove the existence of God. And perhaps it never will. You see, there are limitations to logical evidence, to the cold, hard facts that science provides. In order to truly embrace the beauty and mystery of life, we must also embrace our emotions and relationships.

To understand the beauty and mystery of life, we must first consider the different perspectives on the existence of God and the role of science in understanding our world. Some believe that life is merely a temporary and transient experience, while others see it as a profound journey filled with profound meaning. It is this very belief that gives life its allure, its sense of wonder and enchantment.

Life's ephemeral nature is what gives it its beauty and mystery. We are here for but a brief moment, like shooting stars streaking across the night sky. And it is this brevity that makes life all the more precious and worth cherishing. Science, with all its empirical evidence, can only scratch the surface of life's complexities. It cannot answer the age-old questions of purpose and meaning. It cannot capture the depths of human emotion and experience.

In contrast to the scientific approach, there is the emotional and intuitive understanding of life's beauty and mystery. It is through our emotions, our connections to others, that we truly grasp the essence of what it means to be alive. Science may explain how the human body works, but it cannot explain the depths of love, joy, and sorrow that we experience. It is through these subjective experiences that we find meaning and purpose.

Take, for example, the story of a young woman who loses her father. She may question the meaning of life, the purpose of her existence. Science may tell her that life is merely a chemical reaction, a series of biological processes. But it is her faith, her belief in a higher power, that gives her solace and comfort in the face of loss. It is in her connection to something greater than herself that she finds meaning and purpose.

Logic and reason are powerful tools, but they have their limitations. They cannot capture the full depth and complexity of human experiences and emotions. To truly understand the beauty and mystery of life, we must embrace our subjective experiences and emotions. We must recognize the importance of nurturing and valuing our emotional connections and relationships.

In our modern world, where logic and reason often reign supreme, it is easy to overlook the transformative power of emotional connections. But it is in our relationships, in the love and support we receive from others, that we find true fulfillment. No amount of logical evidence can provide the same sense of purpose and meaning that comes from deep emotional connections.

So let us not forget the beauty and mystery of life. Let us embrace the ephemeral nature of our existence, and the limitations of science. Let us open ourselves up to the profound joy and sorrow that come from nurturing emotional connections and relationships. In doing so, we will truly understand what it means to live a life of purpose and meaning.

Becoming Your Best Self:
The Transformative Power of Prayer

I look back at my life and to be frank there have been so many times that I've felt worthless; I've often been told that we need to imbibe qualities of people we consider good or admirable, and discard attributes that are evil because they are an unnecessary weight that pulls us down. Many philosophers have debated over time immemorial about the existence of God. However, I feel that we only fully comprehend whether this is true when we have an intimate yet personal revelation. See, the prevailing dogma in a scientific world is that, if we don't have empirical evidence, then something like faith, or the belief in a higher power cannot possibly be true. However, for me, I find my hope in the Christian God. It isn't about being religious or even being someone with high morals, but when we think of life's transient nature; we have to realize that responsibility and growth go hand in hand.

As a kid, I never thought of who my role models were, and consequently, I fell down a rabbit hole where I reasoned that if people thought I was cool, then that meant I was living life well. However, at this time I would like to note that 'living life well' and 'living a good life' are two very different things.

When we approach the concept of the metaphysical I have to speak alongside the backdrop of my faith, because I would rather stay true to my message and honor God rather than dilute my message in an attempt to appeal to everyone, because I know that this is my calling. As a Christian, I differentiate between the 'old-testament' and the 'new- testament' and that is unique to Christians, as they wouldn't be words use by individuals of the Jewish faith because for them there is only one covenant - the 'Tanakh'. However from the Christian perspective the 'Old Testament' is the story of how God brought the world into existence, and what went wrong with it, and how when it went wrong God had a plan. It was that by building a family of 'faith' from one man – Abraham.   The 'Old Testament' shares how the lives of Abraham's descendants commonly known as the nation of Israel did unfold, and the promise that one day a savior or Messiah would emerge and 'break the chains' and set humanity free.

Now, I would urge the reader to allow me the chance to share my perspective – In the pre-Islamic era, the Philosopher Ibn Khaldun put forward the idea of 'assabiyah' roughly translated to 'solidarity' in modern english. However, as a Christian I know that true peace and security comes from God; therefore, I would make the observation that the family of 'faith' is one that is united through 'assabiyah' because family in the truest sense isn't constrained to our technical definition of family, but rather that we connected by our values and beliefs as well as our interests and our passions.

I staunchly believe that we choose our family based on those individuals we trust and respect.

God is good all the time: In Ecclesiastes, we are introduced to a paradox. I would urge both the Christian as well as the atheist to read this book as the way it elucidates the concept of life would point us in the right direction. In life most of us are caught in an unending race; we think doing well in class, having a job that brings us status, or indulging in the usage of drugs to numb the monotony of life would bring satisfaction. However, the wisdom contained within the Bible left me gobsmacked the first time I read it, and I was empowered to understand; I realized that honor and justice go hand in hand. It is because God is just that we need to invite Him into our lives. The idea is that our will and God's plan for our lives are often at odds with each other. Furthermore, being the gentleman that He is; God wouldn't impose His plan for how we should live if we think we want to do things our way. Among those who have turned away from the faith:

1. They turn away from Christianity because they have been hurt by someone who claimed to be a member of the Church.

2. They wonder why it seems like God didn't save them from an event that was quite serious in their perspective.

However, I will say that as humans there is always a chance that we would fall, we could adopt a philosophical approach—to have clear goals, or practice maintaining a journal to be highly aware of our goals and vices—in order to become the best version of ourselves. Yet, I need God to be the best version of myself, and I would be thankful if He heard my prayer and continued to show me the way.

The Power of Conscience

Throughout my journey of exploring the complexities of human existence, I have come to realize the immense power of conscience in shaping our lives. In this subchapter, I aim to delve into the validity of human conscience and underscore the importance of trusting others. While self-reliance through science has its merits, it is vital to recognize its limitations. Instead, I propose that hope and purpose serve as fundamental themes that guide our moral compass and imbue our lives with meaning.

To understand the essence of conscience, we must first explore its historical and philosophical underpinnings. Over the course of history, various interpretations of conscience have emerged, each influenced by cultural and societal contexts. From ancient civilizations to modern philosophies, the role of conscience in moral decision-making and personal integrity has been a subject of deep contemplation.

While history and philosophy shed light on the nature of conscience, it is imperative to delve into the realm of psychological and neuroscientific research to gain a comprehensive understanding. Through careful analysis of cognitive processes, emotions, and social factors, we can unravel the intricate workings of conscience. By examining case studies and experiments, we can begin to decipher the validity and reliability of this internal moral compass.

In an era dominated by scientific advancements, the concept of self-reliance through science challenges the very foundation of conscience. As we prioritize scientific knowledge over moral intuition, we risk dismissing or disregarding the profound wisdom that our conscience offers. It is crucial to critically evaluate the ethical implications of prioritizing scientific progress at the expense of our moral compass.

Trust forms the bedrock of our relationships and social interactions. By placing our trust in others, we not only enhance our own conscience but also validate it. The lack of trust in others can have detrimental consequences, both on a personal level and in terms of societal cohesion. Trust serves as a catalyst for the development of a strong conscience, fostering empathy, compassion, and ethical decision-making.

Hope and purpose infuse our lives with meaning, providing guidance in our moral decision-making. By examining the value and significance of hope and purpose, we can unravel the intricate connection between these existential concepts and the development of a strong conscience. When we have a clear sense of hope and purpose, we are better equipped to navigate the complex terrain of ethical dilemmas.

Education plays a pivotal role in shaping and nurturing a strong conscience. By incorporating moral development theories into the educational curriculum, we can foster trust, instill hope, and imbue purpose in young minds. Teaching empathy, compassion, and ethical decision-making in schools lays the foundation for a society driven by a collective conscience.

In personal relationships, the cultivation of trust and hope is paramount. By adopting strategies and practices that prioritize these essential elements, we can enhance the quality and longevity of our connections. Furthermore, the cultivation of trust and hope serves as a catalyst for the development of a strong conscience, enabling us to make ethical choices in our interactions.

Conscience has the remarkable ability to drive collective action and ignite social movements. Throughout history, we have witnessed the transformative power of individuals who possess a strong conscience, propelling positive change in their communities and beyond. Trust, hope, and purpose are instrumental in mobilizing individuals toward a common goal, fostering unity and progress.

As I reflect on the exploration of the validity of human conscience and the importance of trusting others, I am reminded of the perpetual quest for meaning, purpose, and ethical guidance in life. It is an ongoing journey that necessitates introspection, dialog, and action. By cultivating a strong conscience and fostering trust and hope in society, we can strive toward a world that embraces compassion, empathy, and ethical decision-making.

Chapter 5

The Quest for Truth

Philosophical Questions and Existential Wonderings

In this subchapter, we embark on a journey to delve into the profound philosophical questions that have perplexed humanity since time immemorial—questions that revolve around the very essence of existence and the meaning of life. It is a quest for truth, a search for answers that has driven philosophers, scholars, and thinkers throughout history. As we explore these existential wonderings, we come to realize the importance of this pursuit in our personal growth and understanding of the world around us.

What is the meaning of life?

The age-old question of the meaning of life has captivated the minds of philosophers across cultures and epochs. From ancient Greek thinkers to modern existentialists, countless theories have been proposed in an attempt to unravel this enigma. Some argue that life is inherently meaningless, that we must create our own purpose and find fulfillment within ourselves. Others find solace in religious beliefs, attributing the meaning of life to a divine plan or a higher power. And then there are those who believe that meaning is subjective, shaped by our own interpretations and experiences. As we explore these various perspectives, we gain a deeper understanding of the complexity and beauty of this philosophical question.

Is there a purpose to our existence?

The concept of purpose is deeply intertwined with our existence. We ponder whether there is an inherent purpose to our being, whether we are meant to fulfill a particular role or follow a predetermined path. Philosophical views on purpose diverge, ranging from teleological theories that suggest a grand design guiding our lives, to nihilistic perspectives that assert the absence of any intrinsic purpose. By examining these diverse viewpoints, we grapple with the fundamental question of why we are here and what it means to find purpose in a seemingly chaotic world.

How do our beliefs shape our reality?

Our beliefs form the lens through which we perceive and interact with the world. They shape our reality, influencing our thoughts, actions, and decisions. But how do these beliefs come to be? The role of confirmation bias and cognitive dissonance cannot be ignored in understanding the formation and reinforcement of our beliefs. We find ourselves inclined to seek out information that aligns with our existing beliefs, while dismissing or ignoring evidence that challenges our worldview. As we explore this intricate relationship between belief and reality, we come face to face with the complexities of human perception and the power of our own minds.

Consciousness and self-awareness are deeply profound and philosophical topics that have fascinated thinkers for centuries. What is consciousness? How do we become aware of ourselves and our surroundings? These questions give rise to the mind-body problem, a perplexing philosophical conundrum that explores the relationship between the physical body and the intangible mind. Theories of consciousness range from the idea that it emerges from complex neural activity to the notion that it is a fundamental aspect of the universe itself. As we delve into this realm of philosophical inquiry, we confront the mysteries of our own existence and the boundaries of human knowledge.

Does free will exist?

The debate surrounding free will and determinism has intrigued philosophers, scientists, and theologians alike. On one hand, some argue that our actions are predetermined by a chain of cause and effect, rendering free will an illusion. On the other hand, proponents of free will contend that we possess the ability to make conscious choices and shape our own destinies. This philosophical dilemma raises profound questions about personal agency and responsibility. By delving into the arguments and theories that underpin this debate, we grapple with the nature of human autonomy and the limits of our control over our own lives.

The existence of evil and suffering in the world poses a profound philosophical dilemma. How can we reconcile the presence of immense suffering with the notion of a benevolent and all-powerful deity? This question has given rise to various theological responses, such as theodicy, which attempts to provide explanations for the existence of evil in a world created by a loving God. Additionally, existentialist thinkers grapple with the human experience of suffering and seek to find meaning in the face of adversity. By engaging with these perspectives, we confront the darkest corners of human existence and the complexities of reconciling our beliefs with the harsh realities of the world.

Ethics and moral responsibility are intricately linked to the meaning of life. They shape our actions and guide our decisions, influencing the way we interact with others and the world at large. Different ethical theories, such as consequentialism and deontology, offer frameworks for understanding our moral obligations. By exploring these theories, we delve into the complexities of navigating ethical dilemmas and seek to understand the interplay between our moral responsibilities and the search for meaning in our lives.

At the heart of philosophical questions about existence and the meaning of life lies the pursuit of truth. It is through this search for truth that we come to understand ourselves and the world around us. Personal growth and self-reflection play a vital role in navigating the labyrinthine pathways of existential wondering. By engaging in self-reflection and embracing personal growth, we embark on a journey of self-discovery, finding meaning in the quest for truth and the development of our own authentic selves.

Throughout history, philosophical questions about existence and the meaning of life have had a profound impact on societies and cultures. They have shaped our beliefs, institutions, and systems of thought. From the ancient Greek philosophers who laid the groundwork for Western civilization to the existentialist thinkers who challenged societal norms, these questions have influenced the course of human history. In the contemporary world, these philosophical inquiries remain relevant, offering individuals and communities the opportunity to explore the depths of their own existence and reshape the narratives that define our collective consciousness.

Each paragraph in this breakdown provides a detailed exploration of a specific aspect of philosophical questions and existential wonderings. By immersing ourselves in these philosophical inquiries, we embark on a transformative journey of self-discovery, personal growth, and the quest for truth. In the pursuit of answers, we come to appreciate the significance of addressing these fundamental questions in our lives and the impact they have on both individuals and societies as a whole.

The Power of Thoughts

Our thoughts have the power to shape our lives in ways we may not even realize. In this subchapter, we will dive deep into examining the impact of our thoughts on our well-being and identity. It is crucial to understand the power of thoughts because they can either be our greatest allies or our worst enemies.

Well-being encompasses various dimensions, including physical, mental, and emotional aspects. Our thoughts play a significant role in each of these dimensions, influencing our overall well-being. Positive thoughts can contribute to a healthy body, a clear mind, and emotional stability. On the other hand, negative thoughts can hinder our well-being, leading to physical ailments, mental distress, and emotional turmoil.

Our thoughts shape our sense of self and identity. The internal narratives we create and the self-talk we engage in play a crucial role in constructing our identity and shaping our perception of ourselves. If we constantly feed ourselves negative thoughts and doubt our abilities, it becomes challenging to develop a strong and positive sense of self. However, when we cultivate positive thoughts and affirm our strengths, we can build a resilient and confident identity.

Hope is a powerful force that can help us navigate challenges and setbacks. Our thoughts, especially positive and hopeful ones, can provide the fuel to maintain resilience and persevere in the face of adversity. By cultivating a mindset of hope and optimism, we can overcome obstacles and find the strength to keep moving forward.

Resilience is closely tied to our thoughts. By cultivating a positive mindset and reframing negative thoughts, we can enhance our resilience and bounce back from challenges more effectively. When we train ourselves to see setbacks as opportunities for growth and view failures as stepping stones to success, we develop the mental strength to face any obstacle that comes our way.

Our thoughts play a significant role in our pursuit of purpose and meaning in life. They can either fuel our motivation and drive or hinder our ability to find and pursue our purpose. When we have a clear and positive mindset, we can align our thoughts with our passions and goals, paving the way for a fulfilling and purposeful life.

Harnessing the power of thoughts requires practical strategies and techniques. Mindfulness, affirmations, and cognitive restructuring are powerful tools that can help us cultivate positive thoughts and rewire our thinking patterns. By practicing mindfulness, we become aware of our thoughts and can choose to redirect them toward more positive and empowering directions. Affirmations allow us to reprogram our subconscious mind with positive beliefs and reinforce a positive self-image. Cognitive restructuring helps us challenge and replace negative thoughts with more positive and constructive ones.

Changing negative thought patterns can be challenging due to ingrained beliefs and habitual thinking. It takes effort and persistence to overcome these barriers. However, by implementing strategies such as self-reflection, challenging negative beliefs, and seeking support from others, we can gradually shift our thought patterns and create a more positive and empowering mindset.

To illustrate the impact of thoughts on various aspects of our lives, I would like to share some case studies and personal stories. These real-life examples will showcase how thoughts can influence well-being, identity, hope, resilience, and purpose. By exploring these stories, readers can gain a deeper understanding and engage more actively with the topic.

In conclusion, our thoughts have immense power to shape our lives. By understanding and harnessing this power, we can transform our well-being, strengthen our identity, maintain hope in the face of challenges, build resilience, and pursue our purpose with unwavering determination. I encourage you to reflect on your own thought patterns and take actionable steps to harness the power of thoughts for your own well-being, identity, and pursuit of purpose. Let your thoughts become your greatest ally in living a fulfilling and meaningful life.

Why Money Doesn't Equal Success

In a world consumed by the pursuit of material wealth, I find it essential to question the belief that money equals success. Society has conditioned me to believe that accumulating wealth and achieving status are the ultimate markers of achievement. But what if I told you that this belief is nothing more than a fallacy? It's an empty promise that leaves us feeling unfulfilled.

True success cannot be measured by the zeros on my bank statements or the possessions I amass. It resides in the intangible aspects of life—the richness of my experiences and the impact I have on the world around me. The danger of prioritizing status over personal fulfillment is that it blinds me to the true essence of success. It traps me in a never-ending cycle of comparison, envy, and discontent, always chasing after the next big thing in hopes of finding happiness.

But here's the truth: No amount of money or status can fill the void within my soul. I may possess all the material wealth in the world and still feel a profound sense of emptiness. I may achieve great success in my career, but if it comes at the expense of my mental and emotional well-being, can I truly call it success?

By placing excessive importance on material wealth and status, I become enslaved by society's expectations. I lose sight of my passions, dreams, and true purpose in life. I sacrifice my authenticity and happiness in exchange for the illusion of success. I forget that success is a deeply personal and subjective concept that cannot be defined by societal norms or external validations.

Moreover, valuing status over personal fulfillment inhibits my ability to form genuine connections with others. When I constantly strive to maintain a certain image or impress others, I build walls around myself, preventing true intimacy and meaningful relationships from blossoming. I become isolated, trapped in a world where appearances matter more than authenticity.

It is vital for me to break free from this mindset and redefine success on my own terms. I must learn to prioritize my inner growth, well-being, and the pursuit of my passions over material possessions. I must embrace the beauty of simplicity and find contentment in the present moment, rather than relentlessly striving for more.

Within the pages of this book, I will be your guide on a transformative journey of self-discovery and self-reflection. Together, we will challenge the societal norms that confine us and explore the true meaning of success. We will uncover the perils of valuing status over personal fulfillment and learn how to cultivate a life of purpose, authenticity, and joy.

It's time for me to break free from the shackles of society's expectations and embark on a path that leads to genuine success and fulfillment. Are you ready to let go of the rat race mentality and embrace a life rich in meaning and purpose? If so, join me on this transformative journey, and together, we will unlock the secrets to a truly successful and fulfilling life.

Embracing the Journey of Life

In today's fast-paced world, it's easy to get caught up in the never-ending race. We're bombarded with messages that success is all about the big bucks, the fancy title, and the shiny achievements. But what if I told you that true success lies not in the end game, but in the ride itself?

Life is a wild journey. It's like a tapestry filled with experiences, emotions, and relationships. It's not just about reaching that finish line; it's about savoring each step along the way. We often forget that life is meant to be lived, not just survived. It's about embracing the present, finding joy in the little things, and cherishing the connections we build with others.

When we get fixated on the final result, we miss out on the magic of the process. We become so focused on our goals that we forget to appreciate the growth, learning, and joy that comes from the journey itself. It's like racing through a garden without taking a moment to inhale the scent of the flowers or feel the warmth of the sun on our skin.

In this book, I'm here to remind you how crucial it is to enjoy the process of life. I want you to slow down, take a breath, and soak in the beauty that surrounds you. Life isn't just about tasks or collecting stuff; it's about finding meaning in every moment.

One of life's gifts is the relationships we build along the way. Whether it's with family, friends, or strangers who enter our lives, these connections add depth to our journey. They remind us that we're not alone, that we're all interconnected.

By nurturing these connections, we create a support system that keeps us sane through life's ride. These relationships give us love, understanding, and a sense of belonging. They bring us laughter, comfort, and memories that make life worth it.

Life is not a race. It's a journey. It's about embracing the highs and lows and finding meaning in every experience. It's about cherishing relationships and living a life bursting with love, purpose, and fulfillment.

So, are you ready to jump on this ride with me? Are you ready to focus on living a life true to yourself? If so, let's embrace the journey of life and uncover the joy that awaits us.

The Role of Money as a Tool

I want to challenge the conventional notion that money is the ultimate measure of success. It's time to shift our focus and recognize money as a tool, rather than a defining factor. Money should enable us to pursue our passions, fulfill our basic needs, and align our lives with our values and desires.

By viewing money as a tool, we can break free from the mindset of accumulating wealth for status or material possessions. Instead, let's use money wisely in pursuit of our dreams. It has the power to fuel personal growth, open up new opportunities, and support causes that resonate with us. By doing so, we can create a meaningful and fulfilling life.

Cultivating Authentic Connections

In today's world, where social media reigns supreme and shallow relationships are formed at the drop of a hat, the importance of fostering genuine and supportive connections cannot be overstated. These connections transcend mere surface-level interactions and acquaintanceships, guiding us toward a life of purpose and fulfillment.

One of the essential elements of cultivating authentic relationships lies in surrounding ourselves with like-minded individuals who share our passions and aspirations. Whether it's a hobby, a career path, or a cause close to our hearts, finding individuals who share our zeal allows us to create a sense of community and support. These relationships serve as a nurturing environment for idea exploration, collaboration, and personal growth. They are the wellspring of inspiration, motivation, and a sense of belonging.

One of the biggest obstacles we face when chasing our passions and dreams is getting our loved ones on board. It's all too common to encounter skepticism, doubt, and even outright resistance from those closest to us. But if we want to succeed, it's crucial to bridge this gap and gain their support. After all, their encouragement can be a powerful driving force in our journey toward success.

The first step is to approach these conversations with empathy and understanding. Remember, our loved ones may have their own fears and concerns, driven by a desire to protect us from potential disappointments or failures. By acknowledging their perspective and truly listening to their concerns, we can create a safe space for open dialog.

Next, we need to articulate our passions and dreams in a clear and concise manner. It's all about developing a compelling narrative that conveys our enthusiasm and dedication toward our chosen path. Sharing personal anecdotes and experiences that highlight our commitment and the positive impact pursuing our dreams will have on our lives can go a long way in getting them to understand our vision.

Another effective strategy is to educate our loved ones about the practical steps we're taking to achieve our goals. Presenting them with a well-thought-out plan that outlines the milestones, resources, and support systems we have in place will demonstrate our preparedness and commitment. This will help alleviate their concerns about the uncertainties of pursuing our passions.

When faced with resistance or skepticism, it's essential to remain calm and composed. Getting defensive or argumentative will only create further tension and hinder effective communication. Instead, respond with patience and understanding. Address their concerns with empathy and provide logical explanations or examples that counter their doubts. This will help them see the validity and potential of our dreams.

Additionally, seeking support from like-minded individuals who have successfully pursued similar paths can be invaluable. Joining communities or organizations related to our passions can provide us with a network of individuals who understand and share our aspirations. Sharing their stories and experiences with our loved ones can serve as powerful anecdotes that further reinforce the validity of our dreams.

It's important to remember that gaining support and understanding may take time. We need to be persistent and patient in our efforts to communicate our passions and dreams. Revisiting the conversation periodically, providing updates on our progress, and sharing any positive outcomes or achievements can help change their perspective and increase their support over time.

Effectively communicating our passions and dreams to friends, family, and loved ones is crucial in gaining their support and understanding. Approaching these conversations with empathy, clarity, and a well-structured plan can bridge the gap of understanding. By remaining patient and persistent, and seeking support from like-minded individuals, we can create a supportive environment that propels us toward success and fulfillment in pursuing our dreams.

Creating a Supportive Community

To truly thrive in our pursuit of passion and purpose, it's imperative that we surround ourselves with kindred spirits who share our ambitions and dreams. These like-minded individuals, who can offer invaluable guidance and motivation, are the key to unlocking our full potential.

One potent way to cultivate a supportive community is to initiate a local meet-up group centered around our specific interests or passions. Through regular gatherings, workshops, and events, we can unite with those who share our fire, creating an environment conducive to collaboration and growth. In addition to forging connections with those who understand our unique journey, these meet-ups offer prime opportunities for networking, resource sharing, and tapping into the wisdom of those who have already achieved great success in their chosen domain.

Another avenue worth exploring is joining established organizations or communities that align with our aspirations and goals. Whether it is a professional association, a volunteer group, or an online forum, these communities provide a treasure trove of knowledge, connections, and support. By actively engaging in discussions, attending conferences or seminars, and participating in group initiatives, we not only expand our network but also expose ourselves to fresh perspectives, ideas, and potentially life-altering opportunities.

Moreover, thanks to the ever-expanding realm of social media, connecting with individuals who share our passions and dreams has never been easier. By strategically employing hashtags, joining pertinent groups or communities, and actively participating in discussions, we can forge valuable relationships with fellow travelers on the same path. These online alliances can pave the way for profound collaborations, mentorship opportunities, and even lifelong friendships.

To cultivate a supportive community, it's vital that we contribute actively and serve as a resource for others. By sharing our skills, knowledge, and experiences, we create a mutually beneficial environment where individuals learn from each other and find solace in times of need. This can take the form of mentoring, organizing transformative workshops or webinars, or simply lending a compassionate ear and offering words of encouragement.

Moreover, nurturing relationships within our community should be a top priority. Attending events, showing genuine interest in others' projects, and fostering a spirit of collaboration are all essential ingredients in building robust connections and fostering a culture of upliftment. By investing in these bonds and forming deep, meaningful relationships, we not only bask in the support of others but also contribute to the creation of a positive and empowering community.

Seeking out or forging communities, networks, or organizations that share and bolster our passions and aspirations is paramount to our quest for fulfillment and accomplishment. Through local meet-ups, professional associations, online communities, and social media platforms, we can establish a network of like-minded souls, gain profound insights, and find the unwavering support and encouragement needed to navigate the treacherous terrain of challenges and obstacles. By actively participating and wholeheartedly contributing to these communities, we not only enhance our own journey but also create an environment where others can flourish and triumph.

The Importance of Finding Balance

Balance is the key to finding happiness and purpose in life. It is the delicate equilibrium between opposing forces that allows us to navigate the challenges and complexities of existence. In our pursuit of happiness, we often find ourselves grappling with the tension between happiness and ignorance. Ignorance may bring fleeting moments of joy, but it ultimately hinders our long-term fulfillment and purpose. To find true balance, we must embrace the role of faith and treat others with kindness and love.

To fully grasp the concept of balance, it is crucial to define the terms that underpin this subchapter. Balance is the state of equilibrium, where various elements coexist harmoniously. Happiness is the subjective experience of joy and contentment. Ignorance refers to a lack of knowledge or awareness. Purpose is the sense of meaning and direction in life. Faith is the belief in something beyond oneself. Kindness is the act of showing compassion and benevolence toward others. Love is a profound feeling of affection and care. It is important to clarify any nuances or misconceptions associated with these terms to ensure a shared understanding.

We will explore the relationship between happiness and ignorance, analyzing how short-term happiness derived from ignorance can hinder our long-term fulfillment and purpose. Additionally, we will examine the impact of faith on finding purpose, recognizing its ability to provide guidance and meaning in life. Finally, we will discuss the significance of treating others with kindness and love, understanding how these actions contribute to personal fulfillment and a sense of balance.

To comprehend the tension between happiness and ignorance, we must recognize that ignorance can provide temporary bliss by shielding us from painful truths or uncomfortable realities. However, it ultimately obstructs our personal growth and prevents us from attaining genuine fulfillment and purpose. In contrast, faith plays a significant role in our quest for purpose. It provides us with guidance, instilling hope and meaning in our lives, even during challenging times. Moreover, treating others with kindness and love fosters personal growth and a sense of balance. By extending empathy and compassion to others, we cultivate deeper connections, enriching our own lives in the process.

While striving for balance, we may encounter challenges and limitations. It is essential to acknowledge and overcome these obstacles to achieve true equilibrium. By doing so, we can improve our relationships, enhance our overall well-being, and attain a profound sense of purpose. The implications of finding balance extend far beyond our individual lives; they ripple into our communities and the world at large, fostering harmonious interactions and inspiring others to embark on their own journey toward balance.

To gain a deeper understanding of the significance of finding balance, there are numerous additional topics and areas of research to explore. For instance, delving into the neuroscience behind happiness and purpose can offer insights into the biological mechanisms underlying these states. Additionally, investigating different spiritual practices and their impact on balance can expand our understanding of faith and its role in achieving equilibrium. These explorations can lead us to new avenues for personal growth and development, unlocking untapped potential in our pursuit of balance.

In conclusion, balance is the linchpin of happiness and purpose in life. By embracing faith and treating others with kindness and love, we can achieve the delicate equilibrium necessary for a fulfilling existence. It is through this balance that we can experience true happiness and find our ultimate purpose. As we embark on this journey, let us reflect on the concepts discussed and apply them in our own lives. By doing so, we can create a more harmonious world filled with love, compassion, and purpose.

Chapter 6

A Universal Context

Internal Luminosity

Internal luminosity, the inner radiance, and authenticity that exist within every individual, is a concept that holds immense significance in personal growth and fulfillment. It is a beacon that guides us toward living our most authentic lives. When we tap into our internal luminosity, we shine from within, attracting opportunities and experiences that align with our true selves. In this chapter, I will explore the factors that contribute to internal luminosity and how we can embrace and nurture it to live a more fulfilling life.

To cultivate internal luminosity, self-awareness is paramount. Understanding our values, passions, and strengths allows us to align our actions and decisions with our authentic selves. When we embrace authenticity, we let go of societal expectations and external pressures, and instead, follow our own unique path. It is this alignment that allows our internal luminosity to shine brightly.

Engaging in activities that bring us joy, fulfillment, and personal growth is crucial in tapping into our internal luminosity. Whether it's pursuing hobbies, learning new skills, or engaging in meaningful relationships, these activities enrich our lives and allow us to connect with our true selves. They become the fuel that ignites our internal luminosity, propelling us forward on our journey of self-discovery.

Imagine waking up with intention and mindfulness, starting your day with practices such as meditation, journaling, or affirmations. These moments of stillness and reflection set the tone for the day, helping us connect with our inner selves and align our actions with our internal luminosity. Throughout the day, we engage in work or activities that resonate with our passions and values, allowing us to feel a deep sense of fulfillment and inner radiance.

External factors can sometimes dim our internal luminosity. Societal expectations, personal setbacks, and self-doubt can cast shadows over our authentic selves. However, there are strategies we can employ to overcome these challenges. Seeking support from loved ones, practicing self-care rituals, and reframing setbacks as opportunities for growth are all ways to reignite our internal luminosity and stay true to ourselves.

As the day comes to a close, it is important to engage in activities that recharge and nourish our inner radiance. Whether it's spending quality time with loved ones, engaging in leisure activities that bring us joy, or practicing self-care rituals, these moments help replenish our energy and remind us of the importance of self-nurturing. They anchor us in our internal luminosity and set the stage for the next day.

Taking the time to reflect on our experiences, emotions, and overall sense of authenticity throughout the day is essential. We can identify the moments that brought us the most joy and fulfillment, as well as areas where we may have felt disconnected from our internal luminosity. This reflection allows us to learn and grow, making adjustments to live a more authentic life each day.

Embracing our internal luminosity not only benefits us as individuals but also has a profound impact on our relationships, work, and overall well-being. When we shine authentically, we inspire others to do the same. Our authenticity becomes a catalyst for positive change, creating a ripple effect that extends far beyond us.

Internal luminosity is a powerful force that holds the potential for personal growth and fulfillment. It is a reminder that each of us has the capacity to shine brightly from within. By embracing our own internal luminosity and living authentically, we unlock a life of purpose, joy, and self-discovery. So let us embrace the journey, for within us lies a radiance waiting to illuminate the world.

The Potency of Empathy

Empathy, a concept often overlooked and undervalued, possesses a potency that is unrivaled in its ability to bridge human experiences, foster connection, and facilitate collective healing on a global scale. In this subchapter, we will delve into the profound impact of empathy, exploring its power through a hypothetical scenario. By immersing ourselves in this scenario, we will gain a deeper understanding of the transformative potential empathy holds.

To truly grasp the power of empathy, we will embark on a journey through a hypothetical scenario. This scenario serves as a powerful tool to illustrate the profound impact empathy can have in our lives. By creating a fictional situation, we can explore the nuances of empathy and how it can bring about significant change and understanding.

Picture this: A small coastal town, battered by a devastating hurricane, stands on the precipice of despair. Our characters, Maria and John, find themselves at the epicenter of this struggle. Maria, a single mother, struggles to provide for her children amidst the wreckage left behind by the storm. John, a veteran suffering from PTSD, battles with his own demons as he tries to rebuild his life. This scenario represents a common human experience—the resilience and struggle faced by individuals in the aftermath of a disaster.

As we delve deeper into the hypothetical scenario, we uncover the contrasting displays of empathy. Maria, despite her own hardships, shows empathy toward John, understanding the invisible scars he carries. John, on the other hand, initially lacks empathy toward Maria's struggles, consumed by his own pain. By examining the potential impact of empathy in this scenario, we begin to understand how it can transform the characters' lives and the situations they find themselves in.

Empathy serves as a bridge, connecting individuals who may have vastly different experiences. In the hypothetical scenario, Maria's empathy for John creates a connection that leads to understanding, support, and ultimately growth. Through this connection, they both find solace and strength in each other's experiences, reinforcing the transformative power of empathy in fostering human connection.

Empathy goes beyond individual connections; it plays a pivotal role in facilitating collective healing on a global scale. Throughout history, we have witnessed how empathy has been instrumental in resolving conflicts, promoting peace, and addressing societal issues. By examining real-world examples, such as the Truth and Reconciliation Commission in South Africa or the restorative justice movement, we gain insight into the potential of empathy to contribute to collective healing.

The hypothetical scenario allows us to distill valuable lessons and insights. We learn that empathy, when cultivated and applied, has the potential to transform lives. By immersing ourselves in the experiences of others and striving to understand their struggles, we can promote empathy and healing in our own lives and those around us.

Empathy plays a crucial role in building empathetic communities. When communities prioritize empathy, they create a supportive and inclusive environment that fosters understanding and compassion. Through empathy, we can cultivate a sense of belonging, where individuals feel seen, heard, and valued.

Empathy can be leveraged as a powerful tool for social change. When individuals and communities are motivated by empathy, they are driven to take action and create positive societal transformations. By empathizing with those who are marginalized or oppressed, we can challenge the status quo and work toward a more just and equitable society.

The potential global impact of empathy is vast. Empathy has the power to bridge divides, address global challenges, and promote peace and understanding among different cultures and nations. By fostering empathy on a global scale, we can create a world where compassion and understanding reign, paving the way for a brighter future.

In conclusion, empathy holds immense potency in bridging human experiences, fostering connection, and facilitating collective healing. Through the exploration of a hypothetical scenario, we have seen how empathy can transform lives and contribute to positive change. By prioritizing empathy in our own lives and communities, we can build a more compassionate and understanding world, one connection at a time.

Embracing the Journey

Embracing the journey is a concept that has profoundly impacted my life. It is about understanding that life is not just about reaching the destination, but about fully experiencing and appreciating the process of getting there. It is about embracing the ups and downs, the challenges and triumphs, and recognizing that each step along the way contributes to our personal growth and empowerment.

For me, embracing the journey is deeply connected to the transformative power of divine love. It is about understanding that we are all on a path of personal growth and empowerment, and that divine love is the catalyst for this transformation. When we embrace the journey with an open heart and a willingness to learn and grow, we allow divine love to guide us and support us along the way.

Self-doubt is something that can often hinder our personal journeys. It is that nagging voice in our heads that tells us we are not good enough or capable enough to achieve our goals. It is a powerful force that can hold us back from reaching our full potential. Understanding self-doubt and its effects is crucial in order to overcome it and continue on our journey toward personal growth and empowerment.

Recognizing the uniqueness of our own journeys is also essential. Each of us has a distinct path to follow, and embracing this individuality can lead to great personal growth and empowerment. It is about acknowledging that our journey is not meant to be compared to others but rather celebrated for its own unique qualities. When we embrace our distinct journey, we allow ourselves to fully experience the lessons and opportunities that come our way.

Shedding self-doubt and embracing divine love are two strategies that can help us on our journey toward personal growth and empowerment. Self-reflection and positive affirmations are powerful tools that can help us overcome self-doubt and replace it with self-belief and confidence. Additionally, embracing divine love and recognizing its transformative power can help us overcome our doubts and fears, and allow us to fully embrace the journey with love and courage.

Challenges are an inevitable part of life, and embracing them can lead to incredible personal growth and empowerment. When we see challenges as opportunities for growth, we shift our perspective and open ourselves up to transformative experiences. It is through these challenges that we learn resilience, strength, and determination, and ultimately become the best version of ourselves.

Faith and spirituality play a significant role in our journey toward personal growth and empowerment. They provide us with a sense of guidance and support and help us navigate through the ups and downs of life. The transformative power of divine love is deeply intertwined with faith and spirituality, as it allows us to connect with something greater than ourselves and find solace and strength in times of need.

Finding meaning and purpose in our journey is essential for our overall fulfillment and satisfaction. It is about understanding that our journey is not just about achieving external success, but about discovering our true passions, values, and desires. When we embrace the journey with an open mind and a willingness to explore and learn, we find meaning and purpose in the most unexpected places.

Cultivating a growth mindset is a fundamental aspect of embracing the journey. It is about adopting a mindset that sees challenges as opportunities for growth, and failure as a stepping stone toward success. A growth mindset allows us to approach our journey with curiosity, resilience, and a willingness to learn and adapt. It is through this mindset that we can truly experience personal growth and empowerment.

Navigating setbacks and failure is an inevitable part of any journey. It is important to develop strategies to overcome these obstacles and learn from them. Setbacks and failure should not be seen as a reflection of our worth or capabilities, but rather as opportunities for learning and growth. Embracing the journey with courage and resilience allows us to navigate these setbacks and come out stronger on the other side.

In conclusion, embracing the journey is about understanding that life is not just about reaching the destination, but about fully experiencing and appreciating the process of getting there. It is about shedding self-doubt, embracing divine love, and seeing challenges as opportunities for growth. It is about finding meaning and purpose in our journey, cultivating a growth mindset, and navigating setbacks with courage and resilience. By embracing the journey, we can truly experience personal growth and empowerment, and transform our lives in profound ways.

Transcending Constraints

As I sit here, contemplating the essence of the human spirit, I am struck by its remarkable potential to transcend constraints and achieve a state of divine empowerment. However, I must relay to you the reader that there is a difference between organized religion and faith. It is that as Christians we know that there is a way we should live. There is a reason we think that is true.

It is that we've often experienced the beauty of life when we live in a way that honors God. Often our purpose doesn't require some gargantuan feat of sheer will and determination; on the contrary, we can start living a purposeful life right where we are. In my exploration of faith, I have realized that as human beings we have a responsibility to ourselves and a duty towards others. As we live life striving to be the best version of ourselves we have a responsibility to take care of ourselves, and pursue something that is good. However, we also have a duty. To transcend constraints means to rise above the limitations that society, history, and our own minds impose upon us. It is the ability to break free from the shackles of societal norms, prejudices, and systems of oppression, and reach for something greater within ourselves. In this exploration of personal growth and self-actualization, we will delve into the historical and social context of constraints, the power of the human spirit, and the role of mindset, belief systems, and culture in this transformative journey.

Constraints, in their various forms, have been deeply ingrained in society throughout history. From oppressive regimes to discriminatory societal norms, these constraints have restricted individuals, stifling their true potential. However, it is through understanding the historical and social factors that contribute to the existence of these constraints that we can begin to dismantle them. By examining the systems of oppression that have shaped our understanding of limitations, we can recognize the need for change and work toward a more inclusive and empowering society.

While constraints may be imposed upon us, the human spirit possesses an inherent strength and resilience that can overcome even the most daunting obstacles. It is within us, waiting to be tapped into, waiting to be unleashed. By connecting with our inner strength, we can defy limitations and achieve greatness. Throughout history, there have been countless examples of individuals who have defied societal expectations and transcended constraints to achieve extraordinary feats. Their stories serve as inspiration, reminding us of the transformative power of the human spirit.

One such example is the renowned physicist, Stephen Hawking. Despite being diagnosed with a debilitating motor neuron disease at the age of 21, Hawking defied the constraints of his physical condition and went on to make ground-breaking contributions to the field of cosmology. His unwavering determination and unyielding spirit allowed him to overcome his physical limitations and reach for the stars, quite literally.

Another example is the incomparable Maya Angelou, whose powerful voice and words continue to resonate with generations. Growing up in a racially segregated society, Angelou faced numerous challenges and setbacks. However, she refused to let these constraints define her. Through her poetry and activism, she brought attention to the struggles of the marginalized and empowered others to rise above their own limitations.

What sets these individuals apart? What enabled them to transcend constraints? It is the unwavering belief in their own potential, the refusal to be defined by their circumstances, and the resilience to persevere in the face of adversity. These qualities, when nurtured and cultivated, can propel us toward achieving our own divine empowerment.

The power of mindset and belief systems cannot be overstated. It is through positive thinking, resilience, and determination that we can overcome the constraints that hold us back. By cultivating empowering beliefs and attitudes, we can rewrite the narrative of our own lives and transform our limitations into opportunities for growth.

However, it is important to recognize the influence of culture on the process of transcending constraints. Cultural factors, such as values, norms, and expectations, can either facilitate or hinder our journey toward empowerment. By understanding how cultural practices and beliefs shape our perception of limitations, we can challenge and reshape these narratives to promote personal growth and empowerment.

When we transcend constraints, we not only experience personal fulfillment, but we also contribute to positive societal progress. By defying societal expectations and dismantling oppressive systems, we become catalysts for change. Our achievements and empowerment inspire and motivate others, creating a ripple effect that can lead to a more inclusive and just society.

The power of stories and role models cannot be overlooked in this process. By sharing stories of individuals who have overcome limitations, we instill hope and belief in our own potential. Role models serve as beacons of possibility, guiding us toward our own divine empowerment. It is through the collective sharing of these stories and the visibility of role models that we can foster a culture of empowerment and inspire future generations to transcend constraints.

In conclusion, transcending constraints is not only a personal journey but also a societal imperative. By recognizing and challenging the constraints imposed upon us, tapping into the power of our human spirit, and cultivating empowering beliefs and attitudes, we can achieve a state of divine empowerment. Through this transformative journey, we become agents of change, dismantling oppressive systems and inspiring others to reach for something greater within them. It is through our collective efforts that we can create a world where limitations are shattered and the human spirit soars.

The Power Within

Inner strength is a concept that holds immense power and significance in shaping our destiny. It is the reservoir of untapped potential that lies within each individual, waiting to be unleashed. When we learn to harness this inner strength, we can navigate the trials and tribulations of life with unwavering resilience and determination.

As I reflect on my own journey of self-discovery, I am reminded of the countless times I doubted my own abilities and underestimated the strength that resided within me. It was only through a conscious effort to tap into my inner strength that I was able to overcome seemingly insurmountable obstacles and emerge stronger than ever before.

So, how can one tap into their inner strength? It begins with a shift in our mindset, a recognition of the untapped power that lies dormant within us. By cultivating a sense of self-awareness and embracing our unique qualities and talents, we can awaken this inner strength and embark on a path toward personal growth and fulfillment.

To access and harness this inner strength, it is essential to practice certain strategies and techniques. One effective approach is through the incorporation of practical tips and exercises into our daily lives. These exercises may include journaling, prayer, and visualization, all of which serve to deepen our connection with our inner selves and unlock our full potential.

But why should we bother embracing our unique potential? What are the benefits of such a pursuit?

Embracing our unique qualities and talents leads to personal fulfillment, success, and a profound sense of purpose. When we recognize and celebrate our individuality, we set ourselves on a path toward self-actualization, where we can truly thrive and make a meaningful impact on the world around us.

Yet, self-doubt and fear often plague our journey toward embracing our potential. These common obstacles can cripple our progress and hinder us from realizing our true power. It is crucial to address these challenges head-on and develop strategies for overcoming them. Building self-confidence through positive affirmations, seeking support from mentors, and challenging our limiting beliefs are all effective ways to conquer self-doubt and fear.

Mindset plays a vital role in shaping our destiny. A positive mindset serves as the catalyst for creating our own reality. By cultivating empowering thoughts and beliefs, we can influence our actions and shape the outcomes we desire. It is essential to surround ourselves with positivity, whether through affirmations, gratitude practices, or engaging with uplifting content, to maintain a constructive mindset and unlock our true potential.

Staying motivated and persevering in the face of adversity is no easy feat, but it is crucial in shaping our destiny. By adopting strategies such as setting clear goals, breaking them down into actionable steps, and celebrating small victories along the way, we can maintain motivation and resilience during challenging times. Additionally, drawing inspiration from the stories of others who have overcome adversity can serve as a powerful reminder of what is possible when we persist.

External limitations and societal expectations often impose restrictions on our personal growth and potential. These constraints can stifle our dreams and prevent us from forging our unique path. To overcome these limitations, we must break free from societal norms and embrace our individuality. By challenging the status quo, we can unlock our true power and shape our destiny on our terms.

Finding our passion and purpose in life is an integral part of shaping our destiny. It is through self-discovery that we unearth our deepest desires and align our actions with our authentic selves. By engaging in reflection exercises, exploring our interests and values, and seeking new experiences, we can navigate the labyrinth of self-discovery and uncover our true passion and purpose.

Harnessing our inner strength is not just about personal growth; it is also about making a positive impact on others and the world. When we recognize the power within us, we can use it to effect change and create a ripple effect of positivity. Numerous examples abound of individuals who have harnessed their inner strength to create positive change, inspiring others to do the same.

In our pursuit of shaping our destiny, it is crucial to maintain a balanced approach. Striving for personal growth and success should not come at the expense of our well-being or relationships. It is essential to prioritize self-care, cultivate a healthy work-life balance, and avoid burnout. By maintaining equilibrium in our lives, we can sustain the energy and focus required to shape our destiny while nurturing our overall well-being.

Harnessing our inner strength is an ongoing journey, a continuous process of self-discovery, growth, and transformation. As we tap into this inner power, we unlock a world of possibilities and redefine our destiny. Embracing our unique potential and navigating life with unwavering determination, we can shape a future that surpasses even our wildest dreams.

Chapter 7

Conclusion

Embracing Faith and Empathy

In my journey of exploring the complexities of life and seeking meaning, I have come to realize the profound impact that faith in God and empathy can have on our daily existence. These two pillars, when embraced and nurtured, can transform our lives and the lives of those around us. Faith in God provides us with guidance, strength, and hope, while empathy allows us to understand and share the feelings of others. Together, they form the foundation for a fulfilling and purposeful life.

Faith in God is not merely a blind belief or a set of religious doctrines. It is a deep trust and confidence in a higher power that transcends our limited understanding. Faith empowers us to face challenges and adversities with courage and resilience, knowing that we are not alone in our struggles. It shapes our beliefs, values, and actions, serving as a moral compass that guides us toward a life of integrity and purpose. Through faith, we find solace in times of despair and find strength to persevere in the face of uncertainty.

Empathy, often overlooked in today's fast-paced and individualistic society, is a fundamental aspect of our humanity. It is the ability to understand and share the feelings of others, stepping into their shoes and truly connecting with their experiences. Empathy fosters positive relationships, promoting compassion and understanding. It is through empathy that we can build bridges of understanding and reach out to others in times of need. By cultivating empathy, we can create a more compassionate and harmonious world.

Throughout the ages, numerous works have explored the concept of faith in God from various perspectives. These works offer valuable insights into the nature of faith and its impact on individuals. From religious texts to philosophical treatises, each work sheds light on different aspects of faith and its significance in our lives. By delving into these texts, we gain a deeper understanding of faith's role in decision-making, well-being, and relationships.

Similarly, the importance of empathy has been extensively studied and discussed in various works. Through a careful examination of key texts, we uncover the transformative power of empathy in personal relationships. Research has shown that empathy promotes understanding, forgiveness, and conflict resolution. However, there are also barriers to empathy that need to be addressed. By exploring these barriers and strategies for cultivating empathy, we can enhance our ability to connect with others on a deeper level.

As we integrate the reviewed works, a clear picture emerges of the interconnectedness of faith and empathy. Both faith and empathy revolve around common themes such as love, compassion, and selflessness. Through faith in God, we are able to tap into a source of unconditional love and compassion, which in turn enables us to practice empathy toward others. By embracing faith, we are better equipped to make positive choices that benefit not only ourselves but also the larger community.

In conclusion, the importance of faith in God and empathy cannot be overstated. These two pillars, when embraced and nurtured, have the power to transform our lives and the lives of those around us. Through faith, we find guidance and hope, while empathy allows us to connect with others on a deeper level. By integrating faith and empathy into our daily lives, we can create a more compassionate and harmonious world, fostering positive relationships and promoting understanding.

Living a Purposeful Life

Living a purposeful life is not just about going through the motions or following a set of rules. It is about aligning our actions with our faith and values and finding fulfillment and happiness in the process. This concept is relevant to each and every one of us, as we all desire personal growth and balance in our lives.

Faith and values play a significant role in guiding our purpose in life. When we align our actions with our faith and values, we experience a deep sense of fulfillment and meaning. Whether we find purpose through religion, spirituality, or personal values, it is this alignment that gives us a clear path to follow.

Different faiths and value systems can greatly influence our purpose in life. For some, it may mean dedicating themselves to service and helping others, while for others, it may mean pursuing a specific career or creative passion. Regardless of the path we choose, aligning our actions with our faith and values is what allows us to find true meaning in our lives.

But what is the science behind happiness and fulfillment? The psychology and neuroscience of happiness have shown that purpose and meaning are fundamental to our overall well-being. Studies and research have consistently demonstrated that living a purposeful life leads to increased happiness and life satisfaction.

Positive emotions and gratitude also play a crucial role in our well-being. When we cultivate a sense of gratitude for the everyday moments, we find meaning and purpose in even the smallest of actions. This, in turn, contributes to our overall happiness and fulfillment.

Striving for balance is essential to living a purposeful life. It is about finding harmony between different aspects of our lives, such as work, relationships, and personal interests. When we find this balance, we experience a greater sense of happiness and fulfillment.

Personal growth is another key component of living a purposeful life. It is through continuous growth and development that we can truly align our actions with our values. By engaging in practices such as self-reflection, learning, and setting goals, we can cultivate personal growth and ensure that we are living a purposeful life.

However, aligning our actions with our values can sometimes be challenging. Conflicts and obstacles may arise, making it difficult to stay on the path of purpose. By identifying our values and using strategies such as mindful decision-making and intentional actions, we can overcome these challenges and ensure that our actions are aligned with our purpose.

Finding meaning in everyday life is essential to living a purposeful life. When we approach our daily activities with mindfulness and gratitude, we find purpose in even the simplest of tasks. Whether it is taking a walk in nature, spending time with loved ones, or pursuing a passion, finding meaning in these moments enriches our lives and adds depth to our purpose.

Living a purposeful life not only benefits us, but it also has a positive impact on others. Our purposeful actions create a ripple effect, inspiring and influencing those around us. By contributing to the well-being of others, we not only find fulfillment but also create a better world.

As we continue on our journey of living a purposeful life, it is important to strive for ongoing personal growth and reflection. Through self-reflection and prayer, we can ensure that we are staying true to our purpose and making the necessary adjustments along the way. Resources such as books, podcasts, and mentorship can provide valuable guidance and support in this ongoing process.

In conclusion, living a purposeful life is about aligning our actions with our faith and values, finding fulfillment and happiness in the process. By understanding the importance of faith and values, aligning our actions with our values, and gaining an understanding of who we are through prayer, we are able to overcome obstacles. Furthermore, while thus striving for balance and personal growth, one has to acknowledge at some point that finding meaning in everyday life does not have to do with anything but that we aspire to be a better person every day in the hope that we learn from our mistakes. In this manner, we can live a purposeful life that brings us true fulfillment and happiness.

Continuing the Journey

I remember the moment vividly. It was a cold, rainy day in the middle of the winter, and I found myself standing at the crossroads in my journey of faith and self-discovery. The path ahead was uncertain, filled with twists and turns that I couldn't possibly predict. I felt a mix of excitement and fear, knowing that this moment would define the next chapter of my life.

As I stood there, I couldn't help but reflect on how I had arrived at this point. The road behind me had been paved with both triumphs and failures, moments of clarity and moments of doubt. It had been a hard-knock life, filled with obstacles and challenges that had tested my resolve. But through it all, I had learned the value of perseverance and the importance of never giving up on my dreams.

Now, as I faced this new crossroads, I knew that I had a choice to make. I could stay where I was, clinging to the familiar and comfortable, or I could take a leap of faith and explore new paths. I chose the latter.

Stepping outside of my comfort zone was no easy task. It meant embracing uncertainty and leaving behind the safety of what I knew. But deep down, I knew that growth and transformation could only occur when I was willing to take risks and embrace the unknown.

Embracing challenges became a cornerstone of my journey. I realized that every obstacle was an opportunity for growth and learning. Whether it was a setback in my career or a personal struggle, I learned to view these challenges as stepping stones rather than roadblocks. I saw first-hand how individuals who had faced adversity with resilience and determination had come out stronger and more enlightened on the other side.

Seeking guidance from those who had walked a similar path became instrumental in my journey. I sought out mentors who had navigated their own spiritual and self-discovery journeys and learned invaluable lessons from their wisdom and experiences. Finding a supportive community of like-minded individuals also provided a sense of belonging and encouragement that fueled my journey.

Incorporating spiritual practices into my daily routine deepened my faith and self-discovery. These practices allowed me to quiet my mind and connect with something greater than myself. The benefits were undeniable—increased clarity, peace of mind, and a sense of purpose.

Reflecting on my personal values and beliefs became a crucial part of my journey. I realized that alignment between my core values and my actions was essential for true fulfillment and happiness. I asked myself tough questions, delved into the depths of my soul, and used journaling as a tool for self-reflection.

Cultivating gratitude became a transformative practice in my journey. I discovered the power of shifting my focus from what I lacked to what I had. Nurturing relationships with loved ones and a supportive community became a source of strength and encouragement. I found solace in meaningful connections and the shared experiences of others on similar paths. These relationships provided a safe space for vulnerability and growth.

Embracing change became second nature to me. I learned that life is fluid and ever-changing, and by resisting change, I was limiting my own growth. I looked to stories of individuals who had embraced change and found renewed faith and self-discovery, drawing inspiration and courage from their journeys.

Nature became a sanctuary for me, a place where I could find solace and inspiration. As my journey continued to unfold, I realized that there was always more to discover and explore. I sought out books, podcasts, and workshops that could expand my understanding and practice. The journey of faith and self-discovery was an ongoing process, one that required constant curiosity and a willingness to explore new depths.

In sharing my own story, my hope is that readers will be inspired to embark on their own journey of faith and self-discovery. May they find the courage to step outside of their comfort zones, embrace challenges as opportunities for growth, and cultivate a deep sense of gratitude and connection. May they find solace and inspiration in the beauty of nature and seek out the guidance and support of mentors and a supportive community. And may they continue to expand their journey, always hungry for new experiences and insights.

www.ingramcontent.com/pod-product-compliance
Lightning Source LLC
Chambersburg PA
CBHW031411150726
47989CB00002B/612